Betty Crocker

LOW-CARB LIFESTYLE COOKBOOK

Easy and Delicious Recipes to Trim Carbs and Fat

WILEY

Wiley Publishing, Inc.

Library of Congress Cataloging-in-Publication Data:
Crocker, Betty.
  Betty Crocker low-carb lifestyle cookbook.
      p. cm.
  Includes index.
  ISBN 0-7645-8432-4 (paperback : alk. paper)
  1.   Low-carbohydrate diet--Recipes. I. Title: Low-carb lifestyle cookbook. II. Title.
  RM237.73.C76 2005
  641.5'6383--dc22
                      2005000715

Manufactured in the United States of America

10 9 8 7 6 5 4 3 2 1

General Mills

DIRECTOR, BOOK AND ONLINE PUBLISHING: Kim Walter

MANAGER, COOKBOOK PUBLISHING: Lois Tlusty

EDITOR: Lori Fox

RECIPE DEVELOPMENT AND TESTING: Betty Crocker Kitchens

PHOTOGRAPHY AND FOOD STYLING: General Mills Photography Studios

Wiley Publishing, Inc.

PUBLISHER: Natalie Chapman

EXECUTIVE EDITOR: Anne Ficklen

EDITOR: Adam Kowit

PRODUCTION EDITOR: Shannon Egan

COVER DESIGN: Paul Dinovo

INTERIOR DESIGN AND LAYOUT: Holly Wittenberg

MANUFACTURING MANAGER: Kevin Watt

The **Betty Crocker Kitchens** seal guarantees success in your kitchen. Every recipe has been tested in America's Most Trusted Kitchens™ to meet our high standards of reliability, easy preparation and great taste.

FOR MORE GREAT IDEAS VISIT *BettyCrocker*.com

Cover photo: Lemon-Garlic Halibut Steaks (page 150)

Dear Friends,

"Carb-talk" is everywhere these days! If you're interested in trimming carbs and eating a healthy, balanced diet, *Betty Crocker Low-Carb Lifestyle Cookbook* shows you how. Not only are the recipes moderate in carbs and calories, they're low fat, too!

Healthy Hints for a Carb-Counting Lifestyle will help you navigate the best way to cut carbs without eliminating them. Look for information on how to maintain a balanced diet that includes whole grains, keep an eye on portions and get active. If you're planning a menu or a shopping list, or just thinking about what to eat, check out all the great charts like "Carb-Wise" that provides carb, fat and calorie counts for common foods, Carb-Smart Snacks and Desserts and more. The Recipe Browser was created to offer an at-a-glance list of total carbs for every recipe in the book—and the recipes are listed in order from the lowest to the highest carb count!

With 150 great-tasting recipes, you can cut carbs without cutting corners on taste or nutrition. Enjoy succulent main courses like Honey-Mustard Pork Chops, tempting appetizers like crunchy Shrimp Nacho Bites and comforting Whole Wheat Waffles. When dinner calls on busy nights, look for recipes marked ◖ super express, which can be made in 30 minutes or less. Each recipe highlights total and net carbs in addition to complete nutrition information, and many recipes have "Carb-Bits" tips with information ranging from carb facts to serving suggestions and substitutions.

With *Betty Crocker Low-Carb Lifestyle Cookbook*, you'll find plenty of ways to kick up the flavor without kicking up the carbs!

Warmly,

Betty Crocker

Beef Stew, Bologna Style

low-carb *lifestyle*
Table of Contents

Healthy Hints for a Carb-Counting Lifestyle 6

In the News 10

1 Appetizers and Snacks **11**

2 Breakfast Favorites **49**

3 Simply Meat **69**

4 Chicken and Turkey **107**

5 Fish and Seafood **147**

6 Easy Vegetarian **169**

7 Side Dish Sampler **189**

Carb-Counter's Charts 210

Recipe Browser 216

Helpful Nutrition and Cooking Information 218

Metric Conversion Chart 220

Index 221

Healthy Hints for a Carb-Counting Lifestyle

Choosing a healthy lifestyle has many positive benefits and rewards for you and your family. Some people choose to start by making small steps, and others can leap forward at full steam. Whichever method suits you best, the information, charts and recipes in this book will help you navigate the road ahead.

Over the past couple of years, more people have been eating fewer carbohydrates as a way to lose weight. But what are carbohydrates, and what foods have carbohydrates? Those are good questions, and there is a lot of confusion. All food is classified by three main nutrients: carbohydrate, protein and fat. In broad terms, if the food you are eating is not a protein, like meat or poultry, and it's not a fat, like butter or oil, then you're eating carbohydrates like grains, pasta, rice, fruits, vegetables, milk and sweets. Do we need carbohydrates? We sure do; they're necessary for good nutrition because they give us fuel for the energy our bodies need and provide important nutrients like vitamins and minerals. Eliminating or severely restricting carbohydrates results in a body that won't function the way it's supposed to overall.

Because carbohydrates are in many foods, taste so good and are often a comforting treat, they tend to make up a significant part of our diet. If you're considering cutting back on carbs, think moderation, not deprivation. To date, the Food and Drug Administration has established no official definition of "low carbohydrate." Keeping this in mind, you'll be happy to learn that the recipes here fit into a carb-controlled lifestyle yet still provide other important nutrients.

Nutrition was calculated using the following criteria: all main-dish recipes have 20 carbs or fewer per serving and all other recipes are 9 or fewer per serving. As a bonus, the recipes are also low in fat, with main-dish recipes having 10 grams of fat or

fewer per serving and all other recipes having 3 grams or fewer per serving. And, all recipes are 500 calories or fewer per serving and are moderate in sodium (960 milligrams or fewer per serving).

Cutting carbs can help cut calories because food choices can be monitored and limited, but no one food or group of foods will provide the magic solution to weight loss. Additionally, the effects of a low-carb diet haven't been studied over the long term, so the lasting effect on weight or health isn't known, which supports taking a moderate versus restrictive approach.

One of the basic guidelines for good health is to maintain a healthy weight. That can be easier said than done, but the key to weight management has always involved three basic steps: *balanced eating, calorie control* and *exercise*. The bottom line? "Calories in" must equal "calories out," and a calorie is a calorie, no matter where it comes from—including carbs. To lose weight, you need to eat fewer calories and exercise more. Love bread, potatoes, pasta and rice? Enjoy them, but eat them less often and watch portion size—eat just a little less. For example, a side-dish portion of potatoes measures 1/2 cup, and a portion of plain pasta before topping with pasta sauce should measure 1 cup. Sometimes we top our favorite carb foods with higher-fat toppings, like butter on bread, cheese on crackers and sour cream on baked potatoes; the calories from these extras can add up fast. You can reach for them, but choose the lower-fat versions.

The Essential "Four-mula" for a Balanced Diet

Whether or not you are trying to lose weight, Mom was right: you still need to eat a balanced diet. Try to follow these four important strategies.

1

When eating carbs, go for whole grains and fiber to maximize nutrition.

Eat at least 3 servings per day of whole-grain foods, like 100% whole wheat bread, brown rice, old-fashioned or quick-cooking oats, whole wheat pasta and whole-grain cereals like Cheerios®, Wheaties®, Total® and Wheat Chex®. Substitute whole wheat flour for half of the white flour when baking. Whole grains are packed with fiber, important vitamins, minerals and antioxidants. These nutrients are important for a healthy diet.

What's So Great about Whole Grains?

Whole grains have the "whole" package, including all the nutrients and health benefits. Foods made with refined grains lack the bran and germ—and even if the grains are enriched later, only some of these nutrients are put back in. Whole-grain foods include all parts of the grain, and if even one is missing, it's not "whole grain."

- Bran (outer shell)—has fiber, B vitamins and trace minerals
- Endosperm (center)—provides energy in the form of carbohydrates and protein
- Germ (nourishment for the seed)—provides antioxidants

Whole grains come from many sources in addition to wheat and include: amaranth, barley, breads (whole wheat, rye, oat), brown rice, buckwheat, bulgur, cereals (whole grain, whole wheat), quinoa, spelt, steel-cut whole oats, wheat berries and whole wheat flour. But there's more to the story; take a look at how the goodness of grains stacks up:

Nutrient	Source
Fiber	Some grains, like oats, barley, corn and rye, are good sources of soluble fiber, which research shows can help lower blood cholesterol levels.
Folic Acid	Whole-grain foods like ready-to-eat cereals are often fortified with folic acid, a vitamin researchers believe may help reduce the risk for heart disease.
B Vitamins	Release energy from foods, help your body use protein and help support a healthy immune system.
Antioxidants	Whole grains contain vitamin E, selenium and flavonoids, also known as antioxidants. These nutrients protect cells from being damaged by free radicals, which are substances that can make cholesterol more likely to build up inside arteries.
Magnesium	Helps build and maintain strong bones.
Zinc	Helps cells grow and heal.
Phytonutrients	May help protect against chronic diseases.

How Do I Know If It's Whole Grain?

Names like "multigrain bread" or "wheat crackers" give the impression that they're whole-grain products, but a little label spying is in order. Many grain-based products may not contain much, if any, whole-grain ingredients. Here's how to find out if they're really whole-grain foods:

Read the Ingredient Listing: Whole-grain foods list a whole grain—wheat, oats, corn or rice—as the first ingredient. The words "whole" or "whole grain" appear before the grain's name, for example, "whole-grain oats." Also, look for the term "100% whole wheat" or "100% whole grain."

Label Statement: Foods with a high percentage of whole grains are allowed to make this claim on their labels: *"Diets rich in whole-grain food and other plant foods that are low in total fat, saturated fat and cholesterol may reduce the risk of heart disease and certain cancers."*

2 Eat at least 5 servings a day of fruits and vegetables.

Most vegetables have fewer carbs than fruits do, so if you're watching carbs, focus on eating more vegetables. Avoid restricting fruits, however, because they're packed with good nutrients. In fact, fruits are a great alternative to high-fat desserts. Fruits and vegetables are powerhouses of vitamins, some fiber and certain antioxidants.

3 Eat 2 or 3 servings of low-fat dairy each day.

Dairy foods like fat-free (skim) milk and light yogurt are high in calcium, which helps build strong bones and may help burn more fat as part of a high-calcium, reduced-calorie weight loss diet.

4 Eat 2 or 3 servings of lean meat, poultry or fish each day.

Aim for at least 2 or 3 servings of fish each week; fish like salmon and tuna are rich in omega-3 fatty acids, which the American Heart Association recommends as part of a heart-healthy diet. Lean meat and poultry are good sources of protein and have essential iron and zinc. These protein sources don't have carbs but do contribute calories and fat. Learn more about choosing lean proteins in the chart below.

Protein Particulars

Type and Cut of Protein (3 ounces, cooked)	Calories	Total Fat Grams	Saturated Fat Grams
Chicken			
Breast, no skin, baked	150	4	1
Breast, with skin, baked	190	9	2
Thigh, no skin, baked	175	8	2
Thigh, with skin, baked	215	14	5
Drumstick, with skin, fried	200	11	3
Wings, with skin, fried	300	21	6
Nuggets, breaded, fried	285	18	4
Turkey			
Light meat, no skin, baked	145	4	<1
Light meat, with skin, baked	160	6	2
Dark meat, no skin, baked	160	6	2
Dark meat, with skin, baked	180	9	3
Ground, breast	160	6	2
Ground, regular	200	12	3
Beef			
Top round	155	4	1
Eye of round	155	4	1
Round tip	165	6	2
Bottom round	165	6	2
Top sirloin	165	6	2
Top loin	175	8	3
Tenderloin	180	9	3
Pork			
Tenderloin	140	4	1
Loin Chop	180	8	3
Loin Roast	180	9	3

Keep an Eye on Portions

Large portion sizes add up to more calories, so it's helpful to recognize what healthy portions look like and how to have a watchful eye.

To help visualize portions:

- 1 medium fruit or vegetable = size of a tennis ball
- 1 cup = about the size of a woman's fist
- 1 ounce cheese = 2 dominoes or the size of a computer disk
- 1 teaspoon butter or peanut butter = about size of the top of your thumb
- 1 ounce nuts = fits into palm of your hand
- 3 ounces meat = deck of cards or a cassette audiotape
- 1 small banana = size of an eyeglass case

To help control portions:

- Get more "bang for the buck" when eating out. Many entrées are enough to feed two people, so split a meal or take half of it home for the next day.
- Cook at home! It's easier to control portion sizes when you're in charge of making the meal.
- Become an avid label reader. Nutrition labels contain important facts and information on nutrients and serving sizes.
- Check portion sizes periodically; they have a way of creeping up on you. (And watch where extras come from, like the little slice from a row of dessert bars in a pan that you've cut so the row will be even. We like to think it doesn't count, but it does!)

Get Active!

A healthy lifestyle, and successful weight loss, includes keeping physically active. Shoot for at least 30 to 60 minutes of some form of physical activity every day. Rigorous workouts and health club memberships aren't necessary to get results. Here are some ways to fit exercise into your life:

- Park further away from the door.
- Take the stairs and walk up and down escalators when possible.
- Take the long way when walking outside, at your workplace or at the mall.
- Walk airport concourse corridors instead of standing on moving walkways. If you're in a hurry, walk on the walkway!
- Walk during lunch or on breaks.
- Work out with a buddy to keep you motivated.
- Try a new sport to break your routine.
- Play with your kids.
- Walk your dog (or cat!)
- Use fitness equipment at home, like hand weights and an exercise ball.
- Make more trips instead of fewer trips. For example, instead of carrying two bags of groceries into the house at the same time, take in just one bag at a time.

Glycemic Index

In addition to low-carbohydrate diets, you also may have heard of the glycemic index. What is it? The glycemic index is a rating system predicting how high a person's blood glucose levels will rise after eating specific carbohydrate-containing foods. A numbered scale shows which foods cause the highest and lowest raises in blood glucose. Not everyone agrees that the glycemic index is a significant or reliable factor for planning your daily food intake. Most carbohydrate foods aren't eaten alone, and once foods are mixed, the glycemic response in your body may change. Also, the index doesn't take the nutrient content of foods into account.

Volumetrics

The basic principle of volumetrics is that eating less and cutting calories can make you feel hungry and deprived, making weight management more difficult, but by being selective about the types of foods you choose, you can still control calories and feel full while getting the nutrients you need. The theory is that foods with a high water content have a big impact on making you feel full. Examples include fruits, vegetables, low-fat milk, cooked grains (like brown rice and bulgur), lean proteins, beans, soups, stews, casseroles, pasta with vegetables and fruit-based desserts. In addition, fiber can be added to foods for bulk, making you feel more full, reducing calories per portion and lowering "energy density." High-energy-dense foods provide a large number of calories in a small weight, while lower-energy-dense foods have fewer calories for the same weight. For example, for 100 calories, you can either choose 1/4 cup of raisins or 2 cups of grapes; the grapes will make you feel more full.

Carb-Swap!

Decisions, decisions. If you're looking for easy ways to swap out some of the foods and beverages you love, check out these easy options.

Original Options	Swapping Options
Barbecue sauce	Sugar-free barbecue sauce or Dijon mustard
Cereal, sweetened	Whole wheat or whole-oat cereal
Chai drink with milk	Chai-flavored tea without milk
Cheeseburger	93% lean ground beef and low-fat cheese between iceberg lettuce leaves
Crackers, cheese or buttery	Whole-grain low-fat crackers or mini rice cakes
Cream of wheat hot cereal	Old-fashioned or quick-cooking oatmeal
Hard candy	Sugar-free hard candy
Hot chocolate mix w/mini marshmallows	Sugar-free hot chocolate mix
Ketchup	Sugar-free ketchup or Dijon mustard
Lemonade, sweetened	Sugar-free lemonade
Mocha latte	Sugar-free skinny mocha latte

Original Options	Swapping Options
Nachos	Bell Pepper Nachos, page 38
Pasta, regular	Whole wheat or whole wheat blend pasta
Smoothie, fruit, regular	Make with fat-free plain yogurt, frozen unsweetened fruit, fat-free milk and artificial sweetener
Sugar, granulated	Artificial sweetener
Thai chicken wrap (in tortilla)	Wrap filling in lettuce leaves
Turkey and cheese sandwich with mayonnaise	Turkey, mustard or low-fat mayo and low-fat cheese rolled in lettuce leaves
White bread	100% whole wheat bread
White or blush wine	Half wine mixed with half sparkling water
White rice	Brown or wild rice

1 Appetizers and Snacks

Gingered Shrimp   12

Avocado-Seafood Appetizer Bites   14

Easy Salmon Pâté   15

Fresh Basil-Wrapped Cheese Balls   16

Nacho Cheese Pinwheels   18

Greek Appetizer Tarts   20

Corn and Olive Spread   21

Hummus   22

Pineapple-Lime Fruit Dip   23

Maple-Glazed Chicken Kabobs   24

Chicken Satay   25

Chicken-Ham Bites   26

Bacon-Turkey Bites   28

Zippy Chicken Drummies   29

Spicy Meatballs   30

Surf and Turf Kabobs   31

Spiced Pork Tenderloin Crostini   32

Thai-Spiced Cocktail Shrimp   33

Shrimp Nacho Bites   34

Gorgonzola- and Hazelnut-Stuffed
    Mushrooms   35

Sautéed Olives   36

Bell Pepper Nachos   38

Parmesan Puffs with Marinara   39

Layered Vegetable and Aioli Appetizer   40

Spinach Quesadillas
    with Feta Cheese   42

Sun-Dried Tomato and Bacon
    Bruschetta   43

Red Pepper Bruschetta   44

Blue Cheese and Pear Triangles   46

Asiago Cheese and Artichoke Dip   47

Chipotle–Black Bean Dip   48

◑ = **super express** ready in 30 minutes or less

Total Carbs 0g
Net Carbs 0g

OPt Gingered Shrimp *yuck.*

prep time:
15 minutes

start to finish:
**2 hours
20 minutes**

1 1/2 lb cooked peeled deveined medium shrimp, thawed if frozen

1/4 cup soy sauce

2 teaspoons chopped gingerroot

1/4 cup white vinegar

2 tablespoons sugar

2 tablespoons sake or apple juice

1 1/2 teaspoons salt

2 or 3 medium green onions, thinly sliced (2 to 3 tablespoons)

1 In 11×7-inch glass or plastic container, arrange shrimp in single layer. In 1-quart saucepan, heat soy sauce to boiling over high heat. Stir in gingerroot; reduce heat to medium. Simmer uncovered about 5 minutes or until liquid is reduced by half. Stir in vinegar, sugar, sake and salt; pour over shrimp. Cover and refrigerate 2 to 3 hours.

2 Remove shrimp from marinade with slotted spoon; arrange on serving plate. Discard marinade. Sprinkle onions over shrimp. Serve shrimp with toothpicks.

1 shrimp: Cal. 20 (Cal. from Fat 0); Fat 0g (Sat. fat 0g); Chol. 30mg; Sodium 210mg; Net Carbohydrate 0g; Carbs. 0g (Fiber 0g); Pro. 3g | **% daily value:** Vit. A 0%; Vit. C 0%; Calc. 0%; Iron 4% | **exchanges:** 1/2 Very Lean Meat | **CARB. CHOICES:** 0

Gingered Shrimp

24 servings

Avocado-Seafood Appetizer Bites

1 Pt. *yuck*

1 ripe avocado, pitted, peeled and cut into chunks

3 tablespoons mayonnaise or salad dressing

2 teaspoons lime juice

Dash of ground red pepper (cayenne)

Dash of salt

2 large cucumbers, cut into 3/8-inch slices (24 slices)

1 package (8 oz) refrigerated flake-style imitation crabmeat

Fresh cilantro leaves, if desired

1 In food processor or blender, place avocado, mayonnaise, lime juice, red pepper and salt. Cover and process until smooth. (Or if you prefer, blend by hand.)

2 Spread avocado mixture on each cucumber slice. Top with crabmeat. Sprinkle with cilantro. Serve immediately.

1 serving: Cal. 35 (Cal. from Fat 25); Fat 2.5g (Sat. fat 0g); Chol. 0mg; Sodium 100mg; Net Carbohydrate 2g; Carbs. 2g (Fiber 0g); Pro. 2g | **% daily value:** Vit. A 0%; Vit. C 4%; Calc. 0%; Iron 0% | **exchanges:** 1/2 Fat | **CARB. CHOICES:** 0

Easy Salmon Pâté yuck

1Pt.

1 package (8 oz) fat-free cream cheese, softened

1 can (14.75 oz) red or pink salmon, drained, flaked

3 tablespoons finely chopped red onion

2 tablespoons chopped fresh or 1/4 teaspoon dried dill weed

1 tablespoon Dijon mustard

2 tablespoons capers

Assorted whole wheat crackers or pumpernickel cocktail bread, if desired

1 Line 2-cup bowl or mold with plastic wrap. In medium bowl, beat cream cheese with electric mixer on medium speed until smooth. Stir in salmon, 2 tablespoons of the red onion, 1 tablespoon of the dill weed and the mustard. Spoon into bowl lined with plastic wrap, pressing firmly. Cover and refrigerate at least 2 hours but no longer than 24 hours.

2 Place serving plate, upside down, on bowl. Turn bowl and plate over; remove bowl and plastic wrap. Garnish pâté with remaining 1 tablespoon red onion, 1 tablespoon dill weed and the capers. Serve with crackers.

Total Carbs **1g**
Net Carbs **1g**

prep time:
15 minutes

start to finish:
2 hours
15 minutes

carb-bit

Even whole wheat crackers, with their complex carbs, can be loaded with fat. If you want to see how much fat is in a cracker but don't have the box, rub it with a paper napkin. Crackers that leave grease marks are probably high in fat, so you may want to eat them in small amounts.

1 serving: Cal. 50 (Cal. from Fat 15); Fat 2g (Sat. fat 0.5g); Chol. 15mg; Sodium 270mg; Net Carbohydrate 1g; Carbs. 1g (Fiber 0g); Pro. 7g | **% daily value:** Vit. A 4%; Vit. C 0%; Calc. 8%; Iron 0% | **exchanges:** 1 Lean Meat | **CARB. CHOICES:** 0

Fresh Basil-Wrapped Cheese Balls

Total Carbs **0g**
Net Carbs **0g**

prep time:
15 minutes

start to finish:
45 minutes

woulen't make again (the filling is yummy though, on a spread!)

1/2 cup mascarpone cheese (4 oz)*

1/2 cup crumbled **Gorgonzola** cheese (2 oz)

2 tablespoons grated **Parmesan** cheese

1/8 teaspoon pepper

24 fresh basil leaves, 2 to 2 1/2 inches long

1 In small bowl, mix cheeses and pepper until blended. Cover and refrigerate about 30 minutes or until firm enough to shape into balls.

2 Shape 1 1/2 teaspoons cheese mixture into a ball. Roll slightly to form an oval, about 1 inch long. Place on wide end of basil leaf; roll up. Roll leaf and cheese between fingers to form an oval. Repeat with remaining cheese mixture and basil leaves.

3 Serve immediately, or cover with plastic wrap and refrigerate until ready to serve but no longer than 24 hours.

4 ounces cream cheese, softened, can be substituted for the mascarpone.

I serving: Cal. 30 (Cal. from Fat 25); Fat 3g (Sat. fat 1.5g); Chol. 10mg; Sodium 45mg; Net Carbohydrate 0g; Carbs. 0g (Fiber 0g); Pro. 1g | **% daily value:** Vit. A 2%; Vit. C 0%; Calc. 2%; Iron 0% | **exchanges:** 1/2 Fat | **CARB. CHOICES:** 0

Fresh Basil-Wrapped Cheese Balls

Nacho Cheese Pinwheels

Yummy! but very small serving size

1 pt.

4 spinach-flavor, tomato-flavor or plain flour tortillas (8 to 10 inch)

1/2 cup bean dip (from 9-oz can)

1/2 cup jalapeño-flavored cheese dip

3 to 4 tablespoons chopped green onions or chopped fresh cilantro

1 Spread each tortilla with about 2 tablespoons bean dip and 2 tablespoons cheese dip. Sprinkle each with onions.

2 Tightly roll up tortillas; wrap individually in plastic wrap. Refrigerate at least 1 hour but no longer than 24 hours. To serve, cut off ends from each roll and discard. Cut rolls into 1/2- to 3/4-inch slices. Secure with toothpicks if desired.

1 serving: Cal. 25 (Cal. from Fat 10); Fat 1g (Sat. fat 0.5g); Chol. 0mg; Sodium 65mg; Net Carbohydrate 3g; Carbs. 3g (Fiber 0g); Pro. 0g | **% daily value:** Vit. A 0%; Vit. C 0%; Calc. 0%; Iron 0% | **exchanges:** Free | **CARB. CHOICES:** 0

Nacho Cheese Pinwheels

Greek Appetizer Tarts

1 Pt. *good!*

prep time:
35 minutes

start to finish:
35 minutes

2 cups frozen cut leaf spinach (from 1-lb bag)

1 container (4 oz) sun-dried tomato spreadable cheese

1/4 cup crumbled reduced-fat feta cheese

1 package (2.1 oz) frozen mini fillo dough shells (15 shells)

1 medium red bell pepper, if desired

2 tablespoons finely chopped walnuts, pistachio nuts or pecans

1 In microwavable dish, place spinach. Microwave uncovered on High 3 to 4 minutes or just until tender. Drain; press with paper towels to remove moisture. In medium bowl, mix spinach, spreadable cheese and feta cheese until blended.

2 Spoon generous teaspoonful spinach mixture into each fillo shell.

3 Cut star shapes from bell pepper, using sharp knife or small canapé cutter. Sprinkle walnuts over tops of tarts. Place bell pepper star slightly upright on each tart. Serve immediately, or refrigerate until ready to serve.

1 tart: Cal. 50 (Cal. from Fat 30); Fat 3g (Sat. fat 1.5g); Chol. 10mg; Sodium 105mg; Net Carbohydrate 4g; Carbs. 4g (Fiber 0g); Pro. 2g ‖ **% daily value:** Vit. A 25%; Vit. C 0%; Calc. 4%; Iron 2% ‖ **exchanges:** 1/2 High-Fat Meat ‖ **CARB. CHOICES:** 0

About 32 servings (2 tablespoons each)

Corn and Olive Spread yuck   1pt.

Total Carbs **4g**
Net Carbs **4g**

prep time:
5 minutes

start to finish:
5 minutes

2 packages (8 oz each) fat-free cream cheese, softened

1 package (1 oz) ranch dressing mix

1 medium red bell pepper, chopped (1 cup)

1 can (4.25 oz) chopped ripe olives, drained

1 can (11 oz) whole kernel corn, drained

1 can (4.5 oz) chopped green chiles, drained

Tortilla chips, if desired

1 In large bowl, beat cream cheese and dressing mix (dry) with spoon until smooth.

2 Stir in remaining ingredients except tortilla chips. Serve with tortilla chips.

1 serving: Cal. 30 (Cal. from Fat 5); Fat 0.5g (Sat. fat 0g); Chol. 0mg; Sodium 250mg; Net Carbohydrate 4g; Carbs. 4g (Fiber 0g); Pro. 3g | **% daily value:** Vit. A 10%; Vit. C 15%; Calc. 4%; Iron 0% | **exchanges:** 1/2 Skim Milk | **CARB. CHOICES:** 0

super *express*

Total Carbs **8g**
Net Carbs **6g**

prep time:
10 minutes

start to finish:
10 minutes

Hummus *yuck*

1pt.

I can (15 to 16 oz) garbanzo beans,
drained, liquid reserved

1/2 cup sesame seed

I clove garlic, cut in half

3 tablespoons lemon juice

I teaspoon salt

Chopped fresh parsley

Whole wheat pita bread wedges, whole
wheat crackers or raw vegetables, if
desired

1 In blender or food processor, place reserved bean liquid, sesame seed and
garlic. Cover and blend on high speed until mixed.

2 Add beans, lemon juice and salt. Cover and blend on high speed, stopping blender occasionally to scrape sides if necessary, until uniform
consistency.

3 Spoon hummus into serving dish. Garnish with parsley. Serve with pita
bread wedges.

I serving: Cal. 70 (Cal. from Fat 30); Fat 3g (Sat. fat 0g); Chol. 0mg; Sodium 180mg; Net Carbohydrate 6g;
Carbs. 8g (Fiber 2g); Pro. 3g | **% daily value:** Vit. A 0%; Vit. C 0%; Calc. 0%; Iron 6% | **exchanges:** 1/2
Starch, 1/2 Fat | **CARB. CHOICES:** 1/2

12 servings (2 tablespoons dip and 2 apple slices each)

Pineapple-Lime Fruit Dip

1 can (8 oz) crushed pineapple in juice, well drained

1 cup reduced-fat sour cream

1 tablespoon packed brown sugar

1 teaspoon grated fresh lime peel

2 apples, each cut into 12 slices

Total Carbs 8g
Net Carbs 8g

prep time:
15 minutes

start to finish:
15 minutes

1 In small bowl, mix all ingredients except apples.

2 Cover and refrigerate dip until serving. Serve with apple slices.

1 serving: Cal. 60 (Cal. from Fat 25); Fat 2.5g (Sat. fat 1.5g); Chol. 10mg; Sodium 10mg; Net Carbohydrate 8g; Carbs. 8g (Fiber 0g); Pro. 0g | **% daily value:** Vit. A 2%; Vit. C 6%; Calc. 2%; Iron 0% | **exchanges:** 1/2 Fruit, 1/2 Fat | **CARB. CHOICES:** 1/2

Maple-Glazed Chicken Kabobs

IPt.
good

1/2 lb boneless skinless chicken breast halves

3 tablespoons reduced-calorie maple-flavored syrup

2 tablespoons lemon juice

1 tablespoon butter or margarine, melted

1 1/2 teaspoons chopped fresh or 1/2 teaspoon ground sage leaves

1 teaspoon grated lemon peel

1/4 teaspoon pepper

1 medium bell pepper, cut into 16 pieces

1 medium yellow summer squash, cut lengthwise in half, then cut crosswise into 16 pieces

1 Remove fat from chicken. Cut chicken into 24 pieces. In large glass or plastic bowl, mix remaining ingredients except bell pepper and squash. Stir in chicken, bell pepper and squash. Cover and refrigerate at least 4 hours but no longer than 24 hours.

2 Set oven control to broil. Thread chicken, bell pepper and squash alternately on each of eight 8-inch skewers.* Place on rack in broiler pan. Broil with tops 4 inches from heat 2 to 3 minutes; turn. Broil 2 to 3 minutes longer or until chicken is no longer pink in center.

If using bamboo skewers, soak in water at least 30 minutes before using to prevent burning.

Total Carbs 6g
Net Carbs 5g

prep time:
25 minutes

start to finish:
4 hours 35 minutes

1 serving: Cal. 70 (Cal. from Fat 25); Fat 2.5g (Sat. fat 1g); Chol. 20mg; Sodium 30mg; Net Carbohydrate 5g; Carbs. 6g (Fiber 1g); Pro. 7g ‖ **% daily value:** Vit. A 6%; Vit. C 15%; Calc. 0%; Iron 2% ‖ **exchanges:** 1 Vegetable, 1 Lean Meat ‖ **CARB. CHOICES:** 1/2

12 servings

Chicken Satay

2 P
yuck

1 lb boneless skinless chicken breast halves

1/3 cup hoisin sauce

1/3 cup plum sauce

2 medium green onions, sliced (2 tablespoons)

1 tablespoon grated gingerroot

2 tablespoons dry sherry or fat-free chicken broth

2 tablespoons white vinegar

prep time:
35 minutes

start to finish:
**2 hours
35 minutes**

1 Trim fat from chicken. Cut chicken into 1/2-inch strips. In large glass or plastic bowl, mix remaining ingredients. Add chicken; toss to coat. Cover and refrigerate 2 hours.

2 Set oven control to broil. Remove chicken from marinade; drain, reserving marinade. Thread 2 pieces chicken on each of twelve 10-inch skewers.* Place on rack in broiler pan. Broil with tops 3 to 4 inches from heat about 8 minutes, turning once, until chicken is no longer pink in center.

3 In 1-quart saucepan, heat remaining marinade to boiling; boil and stir 1 minute. Serve with chicken.

*If using bamboo skewers, soak in water at least 30 minutes before using to prevent burning.

1 serving: Cal. 80 (Cal. from Fat 15); Fat 1.5g (Sat. fat 0g); Chol. 25mg; Sodium 140mg; Net Carbohydrate 9g; Carbs. 9g (Fiber 0g); Pro. 9g | **% daily value:** Vit. A 2%; Vit. C 0%; Calc. 0%; Iron 4% | **exchanges:** 1/2 Other Carbohydrate, 1 1/2 Very Lean Meat | **CARB. CHOICES:** 1/2

Chicken-Ham Bites

1 Pt.

yuck

2 boneless skinless chicken breast halves, cut into 1/2- to 3/4-inch pieces (36 pieces)

1/2 cup Italian dressing

14 to 16 crimini mushrooms, cut into 1/4-inch slices

6 oz sliced cooked ham (from deli), cut into 1-inch-wide strips

4 fresh basil leaves, finely sliced

1 In shallow bowl, place chicken pieces. Pour dressing over chicken. Cover and refrigerate 30 minutes to marinate.

2 Heat oven to 425°F. Line 15×10×1-inch pan with foil. Spray foil with cooking spray. Place 1 chicken piece on each mushroom slice; wrap with ham strip. Place seam side down (mushroom on bottom) in pan. Drizzle with remaining marinade in bowl.

3 Bake 10 to 12 minutes or until chicken is no longer pink in center. Place basil on top of each bite. Spear bites with toothpicks if desired.

1 serving: Cal. 30 (Cal. from Fat 15); Fat 2g (Sat. fat 0g); Chol. 5mg; Sodium 90mg; Net Carbohydrate 0g; Carbs. 0g (Fiber 0g); Pro. 3g | **% daily value:** Vit. A 0%; Vit. C 0%; Calc. 0%; Iron 0% | **exchanges:** 1/2 Lean Meat | **CARB. CHOICES:** 0

Chicken-Ham Bites

Bacon-Turkey Bites

 1 PH.

Total Carbs **4g**
Net Carbs **4g**

prep time:
25 minutes

start to finish:
**1 hour
10 minutes**

Honey Mustard-Cranberry Sauce

1/2 cup jellied cranberry sauce

2 tablespoons fat-free honey mustard dressing

1/2 teaspoon ground mustard

1 to 2 tablespoons chopped fresh chives

Bacon-Turkey Bites

1 small turkey breast tenderloin (1/2 to 3/4 lb), cut into 1/2- to 3/4-inch cubes

1/2 cup fat-free honey mustard dressing

8 to 10 slices bacon, cut crosswise into thirds

1 In 1-quart saucepan, mix cranberry sauce, 2 tablespoons dressing and the mustard. Heat over low heat, stirring occasionally, just until melted and well blended; cool. Just before serving, sprinkle with chives. Serve sauce warm or cold.

2 In shallow dish, mix turkey and 1/2 cup dressing. Cover and refrigerate 30 minutes to marinate.

3 Remove turkey from marinade; discard marinade. Wrap bacon piece around each turkey piece; secure with toothpick. Place on ungreased broiler pan rack.

4 Broil with tops 4 to 6 inches from heat 8 to 12 minutes, turning once, until turkey is no longer pink in center and bacon begins to look crisp. Serve with sauce.

1 serving: Cal. 40 (Cal. from Fat 10); Fat 1.5g (Sat. fat 0g); Chol. 10mg; Sodium 105mg; Net Carbohydrate 4g; Carbs. 4g (Fiber 0g); Pro. 3g | **% daily value:** Vit. A 0%; Vit. C 0%; Calc. 0%; Iron 0% | **exchanges:** 1/2 Lean Meat | **CARB. CHOICES:** 0

Zippy Chicken Drummies

3 Pt.

wouldn't make again

Total Carbs **4g**
Net Carbs **4g**

prep time:
30 minutes

start to finish:
**1 hour
15 minutes**

Drummies

2 lb chicken drummettes (about 24)

2 tablespoons honey

2 tablespoons ketchup

2 teaspoons red pepper sauce

1 tablespoon Worcestershire sauce

Blue Cheese Dipping Sauce

1/3 cup fat-free small curd cottage cheese

1/2 teaspoon white wine vinegar

2 tablespoons fat-free (skim) milk

1/8 teaspoon white pepper

1 clove garlic, finely chopped

1 tablespoon crumbled blue cheese

Celery sticks, if desired

1 Remove skin and fat from chicken. In heavy-duty resealable plastic food-storage bag, mix honey, ketchup, pepper sauce and Worcestershire sauce. Add chicken; turn to coat with honey mixture. Seal bag and refrigerate at least 15 minutes but no longer than 24 hours, turning occasionally.

2 Meanwhile, in blender or food processor, place cottage cheese, vinegar, milk, white pepper, garlic and half of the blue cheese. Cover and blend on low speed until smooth and creamy. Spoon into serving dish. Stir in remaining blue cheese. Cover and refrigerate until serving.

3 Heat oven to 350°F. Line 15×10×1-inch pan with foil. Place chicken in pan. Bake uncovered about 30 minutes or until crisp and juice of chicken is no longer pink when centers of thickest pieces are cut. Serve with dipping sauce and celery sticks.

1 serving: Cal. 130 (Cal. from Fat 30); Fat 3g (Sat. fat 1g); Chol. 75mg; Sodium 140mg; Net Carbohydrate 4g; Carbs. 4g (Fiber 0g); Pro. 21g | **% daily value:** Vit. A 0%; Vit. C 0%; Calc. 4%; Iron 10% | **exchanges:** 3 Very Lean Meat | **CARB. CHOICES:** 0

Spicy Meatballs

1Pt.

wouldn't make again

Total Carbs **0g**
Net Carbs **0g**

prep time:
35 minutes

start to finish:
**1 hour
5 minutes**

1 lb lean (at least 80%) ground beef

1 tablespoon grated Parmesan cheese

1 teaspoon dried oregano leaves

1/2 teaspoon dried basil leaves

1/2 teaspoon garlic salt

1/2 teaspoon pepper

1 large egg

2 tablespoons lemon juice

1/4 cup olive or vegetable oil

1 clove garlic, finely chopped

1 red jalapeño chili, seeded, finely chopped

1 small onion, finely chopped (1/4 cup)

4 medium tomatoes, chopped (3 cups)*

1 tablespoon dry red wine, if desired

1 In large bowl, mix beef, cheese, oregano, basil, garlic salt, pepper, egg and lemon juice. Shape mixture into 1-inch balls.

2 In 10-inch skillet, heat oil over medium-high heat. Cook garlic, chili and onion in oil about 5 minutes, stirring frequently, until onion is tender. Add meatballs. Cook, turning occasionally, until meatballs are brown.

3 Stir in tomatoes and wine; reduce heat. Cover and simmer 30 minutes, stirring occasionally.

1 can (28 oz) Italian-style (plum) tomatoes, well drained and chopped, can be substituted for the fresh tomatoes.

1 meatball: Cal. 40 (Cal. from Fat 30); Fat 3g (Sat. fat 1g); Chol. 15mg; Sodium 25mg; Net Carbohydrate 0g; Carbs. 0g (Fiber 0g); Pro. 3g | **% daily value:** Vit. A 2%; Vit. C 2%; Calc. 0%; Iron 0% | **exchanges:** 1/2 Medium-Fat Meat | **CARB. CHOICES:** 0

Surf and Turf Kabobs

I Pt.
no

Total Carbs **2g**
Net Carbs **2g**

3/4 lb beef boneless sirloin (3/4 inch thick), trimmed of fat

12 uncooked peeled deveined medium or large shrimp, thawed if frozen and tails peeled

1/2 cup teriyaki marinade and sauce (from 10-oz bottle)

1/4 teaspoon coarsely ground pepper

prep time:
15 minutes

start to finish:
50 minutes

1 Cut beef into 24 (1-inch) pieces. In medium bowl, mix beef, shrimp and teriyaki sauce. Sprinkle with pepper. Cover and refrigerate 30 minutes, stirring frequently, to marinate. Meanwhile, soak twelve 4- to 6-inch wooden skewers in water 30 minutes to prevent burning.

2 Spray broiler pan rack with cooking spray. Thread 1 beef piece, 1 shrimp and another beef piece on each skewer, reserving marinade. Place kabobs on rack in broiler pan.

3 Broil kabobs with tops 4 to 6 inches from heat 5 to 6 minutes, turning once and basting with marinade once or twice, until shrimp are pink and firm. Discard any remaining marinade.

carb-bit

Create Surf and Turf Lettuce Wraps by removing the cooked beef and shrimp from the skewers and serving in lettuce leaves. Lettuce leaves make a great no-carb substitution for tortillas when making wraps.

1 kabob: Cal. 45 (Cal. from Fat 10); Fat 1g (Sat. fat 0g); Chol. 25mg; Sodium 480mg; Net Carbohydrate 2g; Carbs. 2g (Fiber 0g); Pro. 8g | **% daily value:** Vit. A 0%; Vit. C 0%; Calc. 0%; Iron 6% | **exchanges:** 1 Lean Meat | **CARB. CHOICES:** 0

Spiced Pork Tenderloin Crostini

*2 Pt.
wouldn't make again*

prep time:
30 minutes

start to finish:
**1 hour
10 minutes**

1/2 teaspoon seasoned salt

1/2 teaspoon garlic pepper

1/2 teaspoon dried marjoram leaves

1/4 teaspoon ground sage

1 lb pork tenderloin

36 slices (1/4 to 1/2 inch thick) baguette-style French bread (from 10-oz loaf)

1/4 cup Dijon mustard

3/4 cup apple-cranberry chutney (from 8.5-oz jar)

1/3 cup crumbled blue cheese*

Fresh marjoram leaves

1 Heat oven to 425°F. In small bowl, mix seasoned salt, garlic pepper, marjoram and sage; rub mixture over pork. In shallow roasting pan, place pork. Insert meat thermometer so tip is in thickest part of pork. Bake uncovered 20 to 25 minutes or until thermometer reads 155°F. Cover pork with foil and let stand 10 to 15 minutes until thermometer reads 160°F.

2 Meanwhile, reduce oven temperature to 375°F. In ungreased 15×10×1-inch pan, place bread slices. Bake about 5 minutes or until crisp; cool.

3 Cut pork into very thin slices. Spread each bread slice with about 1/4 teaspoon mustard. Top each with a thin slice of pork, 1 teaspoon chutney, about 1/2 teaspoon cheese and marjoram leaves.

Crumbled chèvre (goat) cheese can be substituted for the blue cheese.

1 crostini: Cal. 70 (Cal. from Fat 15); Fat 1.5g (Sat. fat 0.5g); Chol. 10mg; Sodium 190mg; Net Carbohydrate 11g; Carbs. 11g (Fiber 0g); Pro. 5g | **% daily value:** Vit. A 0%; Vit. C 0%; Calc. 2%; Iron 4% | **exchanges:** 1/2 Starch, 1/2 Lean Meat | **CARB. CHOICES:** 1

10 servings (5 shrimp each)

Thai-Spiced Cocktail Shrimp

2 Pt.   good

prep time:
20 minutes

start to finish:
**4 hours
35 minutes**

1 1/2 lb uncooked peeled deveined medium shrimp (about 50)

2 medium green onions, chopped (2 tablespoons)

2 cloves garlic, finely chopped

2 teaspoons grated lime peel

1/4 cup lime juice

1 tablespoon soy sauce

1/4 teaspoon pepper

1/8 teaspoon crushed red pepper flakes

2 teaspoons sesame oil

1 In large glass or plastic bowl, mix all ingredients except oil. Cover and refrigerate at least 4 hours but no longer than 24 hours.

2 Heat oven to 400°F. Spray 13×9-inch pan with cooking spray. Arrange shrimp in single layer in pan. Bake uncovered 10 to 12 minutes or until shrimp are pink and firm. Drizzle with oil. Serve hot.

carb-bit

Shrimp is a lean source of protein, containing only about 100 calories, 2 grams of fat and 0 carbohydrates per 3-ounce serving. To enjoy shrimp at its nutritional best, use a low-fat cooking method like broiling, grilling, baking, microwaving, boiling or steaming.

1 serving: Cal. 80 (Cal. from Fat 15); Fat 1.5g (Sat. fat 0g); Chol. 135mg; Sodium 250mg; Net Carbohydrate 0g; Carbs. 0g (Fiber 0g); Pro. 14g | **% daily value:** Vit. A 4%; Vit. C 4%; Calc. 4%; Iron 10% | **exchanges:** 2 Very Lean Meat | **CARB. CHOICES:** 0

super *express*

Total Carbs **2g**
Net Carbs **2g**

prep time:
15 minutes

start to finish:
15 minutes

24 servings

Shrimp Nacho Bites

1 Pt.

would + make again

24 large corn tortilla chips

1/2 cup black bean dip (from 9-oz can)

1/4 cup thick 'n chunky salsa

24 cooked peeled deveined medium shrimp (about 3/4 lb)

1 avocado, pitted, peeled and cut into 24 slices

1/2 cup shredded Colby-Monterey Jack cheese (2 oz)

24 fresh cilantro leaves, if desired

1 Top each tortilla chip with about 1 teaspoon bean dip, 1/2 teaspoon salsa, 1 shrimp, 1 avocado slice and about 1 teaspoon cheese. Place on cookie sheet.

2 Set oven control to broil. Broil with tops about 5 inches from heat 2 to 3 minutes or just until cheese is melted. Garnish with cilantro leaves. Serve immediately.

1 serving: Cal. 50 (Cal. from Fat 25); Fat 3g (Sat. fat 1g); Chol. 30mg; Sodium 95mg; Net Carbohydrate 2g; Carbs. 2g (Fiber 0g); Pro. 4g | **% daily value:** Vit. A 2%; Vit. C 0%; Calc. 2%; Iron 4% | **exchanges:** 1/2 High-Fat Meat | **CARB. CHOICES:** 0

About 35 mushrooms

good

O Pts.

Gorgonzola- and Hazelnut-Stuffed Mushrooms

Total Carbs **0g**
Net Carbs **0g**

prep time:
30 minutes

start to finish:
50 minutes

1 lb fresh whole mushrooms

1/3 cup crumbled **Gorgonzola** cheese

1/4 cup **Italian-style bread crumbs**

1/4 cup chopped hazelnuts (filberts)*

1/4 cup finely chopped red bell pepper

4 medium green onions, chopped (1/4 cup)

1/2 teaspoon salt

1 Heat oven to 350°F. Remove stems from mushroom caps; reserve caps. Finely chop enough stems to measure about 1/2 cup. Discard remaining stems.

2 In small bowl, mix chopped mushroom stems and remaining ingredients until well blended. Spoon into mushroom caps, mounding slightly. Place in ungreased 15×10×1-inch pan.

3 Bake 15 to 20 minutes or until thoroughly heated. Serve warm.

Walnuts or pistachio nuts can be substituted for the hazelnuts.

1 mushroom: Cal. 15 (Cal. from Fat 10); Fat 1g (Sat. fat 0g); Chol. 0mg; Sodium 60mg; Net Carbohydrate 0g; Carbs. 0g (Fiber 0g); Pro. 0g | **% daily value:** Vit. A 0%; Vit. C 0%; Calc. 0%; Iron 0% | **exchanges:** 1/2 Fat | **CARB. CHOICES:** 0

Total Carbs **1g**
Net Carbs **1g**

prep time:
25 minutes

start to finish:
25 minutes

20 servings (6 olives each)

Sautéed Olives

1 tablespoon olive or vegetable oil

2 tablespoons chopped fresh parsley

1 medium green onion, chopped
(1 tablespoon)

1 teaspoon crushed red pepper flakes

2 cloves garlic, finely chopped

1 cup **Kalamata olives (8 oz)**, drained,
pitted

1 cup **Greek green olives (8 oz)**,
drained, pitted

1 cup **Gaeta olives (8 oz)**, drained, pitted

1   In 10-inch nonstick skillet, heat oil over medium heat. Cook parsley,
onion, red pepper and garlic in oil about 4 minutes, stirring frequently,
until garlic just begins to turn golden brown.

2   Stir in olives. Cover and cook about 5 minutes, stirring occasionally, until
olives are tender and skins begin to wrinkle.

1 serving: Cal. 35 (Cal. from Fat 30); Fat 3.5g (Sat. fat 0g); Chol. 0mg; Sodium 240mg; Net Carbohydrate 1g;
Carbs. 1g (Fiber 0g); Pro. 0g | **% daily value:** Vit. A 4%; Vit. C 0%; Calc. 0%; Iron 4% | **exchanges:** 1/2
Fat | **CARB. CHOICES:** 0

Sautéed Olives

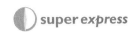

prep time:
15 minutes

start to finish:
15 minutes

6 servings

Bell Pepper Nachos   IPt.

worlent make again

1/2 green bell pepper, seeded, cut into 6 strips

1/2 red bell pepper, seeded, cut into 6 strips

1/2 yellow bell pepper, seeded, cut into 6 strips

3/4 cup shredded reduced-fat Monterey Jack cheese (3 oz)

2 tablespoons chopped ripe olives

1/4 teaspoon crushed red pepper flakes

1 Cut bell pepper strips crosswise in half. In ungreased broilerproof 9-inch pie pan or ovenproof serving dish, arrange pieces close together. Sprinkle with cheese, olives and red pepper.

2 Set oven control to broil. Broil peppers with tops 3 to 4 inches from heat about 3 minutes or until cheese is melted.

I serving: Cal. 50 (Cal. from Fat 30); Fat 3.5g (Sat. fat 2g); Chol. 10mg; Sodium 150mg; Net Carbohydrate 2g; Carbs. 2g (Fiber 0g); Pro. 4g | **% daily value:** Vit. A 15%; Vit. C 40%; Calc. 10%; Iron 0% | **exchanges:** 1/2 Lean Meat, 1/2 Fat | **CARB. CHOICES:** 0

30 servings

Parmesan Puffs with Marinara

1 Pt.
good

1/2 cup fat-free (skim) milk

1/4 cup butter or margarine

1/2 cup all-purpose flour

2 large eggs

3/4 cup grated Parmesan cheese

1 cup marinara sauce, heated

1 Heat oven to 375°F. Spray cookie sheet with cooking spray. In 1 1/2-quart saucepan, heat milk and butter to boiling. Stir in flour; reduce heat to low. Stir vigorously about 1 minute or until mixture forms a ball; remove from heat.

2 Beat in eggs, one at a time, beating until smooth after each addition. Stir in cheese. Drop dough by rounded teaspoonfuls 2 inches apart onto cookie sheet. Bake about 15 minutes or until puffed and golden brown. Serve warm with marinara sauce for dipping.

Total Carbs **3g**
Net Carbs **3g**

prep time:
20 minutes

start to finish:
35 minutes

carb-bit

Marinara sauces are not created equal! Some contain a lot more sugar than others, so check labels for total carbohydrates.

1 serving: Cal. 50 (Cal. from Fat 25); Fat 3g (Sat. fat 1.5g); Chol. 20mg; Sodium 105mg; Net Carbohydrate 3g; Carbs. 3g (Fiber 0g); Pro. 2g | **% daily value:** Vit. A 4%; Vit. C 0%; Calc. 4%; Iron 0% | **exchanges:** 1/2 Lean Meat, 1/2 Fat | **CARB. CHOICES:** 0

Layered Vegetable and Aioli Appetizer

1 Pt.
wouldn't make again

Total Carbs **4g**
Net Carbs **4g**

prep time:
15 minutes

start to finish:
35 minutes

4 oz fat-free cream cheese, softened

1/2 cup fat-free mayonnaise

1 teaspoon finely chopped garlic

1/2 teaspoon grated lemon peel

Dash of ground red pepper (cayenne)

2 medium bell peppers (green, red or yellow), cut into 1 1/2-inch pieces

1 small red onion, cut into 1-inch pieces

1 cup sliced fresh mushrooms (3 oz)

Olive oil–flavored cooking spray

2 tablespoons crumbled chèvre (goat) cheese

2 tablespoons chopped fresh basil leaves

Whole wheat crackers, if desired

1 Heat oven to 450°F. In medium bowl, mix cream cheese, mayonnaise, garlic, lemon peel and ground red pepper until smooth. Cover and refrigerate while preparing vegetables.

2 In medium bowl, mix bell peppers, onion and mushrooms. Spray with cooking spray 2 or 3 times; toss to coat. Spread in ungreased 15×10×1-inch pan. Bake uncovered 15 to 20 minutes or until vegetables are tender; cool slightly. Coarsely chop vegetables.

3 On serving platter, spread cream cheese mixture. Top with vegetables. Sprinkle with chèvre cheese and basil. Serve with crackers.

1 serving: Cal. 30 (Cal. from Fat 10); Fat 1g (Sat. fat 0.5g); Chol. 0mg; Sodium 140mg; Net Carbohydrate 4g; Carbs. 4g (Fiber 0g); Pro. 2g | **% daily value:** Vit. A 15%; Vit. C 25%; Calc. 2%; Iron 0% | **exchanges:** 1 Vegetable | **CARB. CHOICES:** 0

Layered Vegetable and Aioli Appetizer

prep time:
30 minutes

start to finish:
30 minutes

carb-bit

Compare tortilla nutrition labels for total carbohydrate count, or look for products specifically designed for low-carb diets.

16 servings

Spinach Quesadillas with Feta Cheese

IPA.
w would make without

4 fat-free flour tortillas (8 inch)

1/4 cup garden vegetable reduced-fat cream cheese spread

2 cups frozen chopped spinach (from 1-lb bag), thawed, squeezed to drain

1 tablespoon finely chopped red onion

1/4 cup crumbled feta cheese (1 oz)

2 tablespoons fat-free sour cream

Cherry tomato halves, if desired

Sliced ripe olives, if desired

1 Spread 2 tortillas with cream cheese. Layer tortillas with spinach, onion and feta cheese. Top with remaining 2 tortillas; press lightly.

2 Spray 12-inch skillet with cooking spray; heat over medium heat. Cook each quesadilla in skillet 2 to 3 minutes on each side or until light golden brown.

3 Cut each quesadilla into 8 wedges. Top with sour cream, tomato halves and olives. Secure with toothpicks. Serve warm.

1 serving: Cal. 60 (Cal. from Fat 10); Fat 1g (Sat. fat 0.5g); Chol. 0mg; Sodium 170mg; Net Carbohydrate 9g; Carbs. 10g (Fiber 1g); Pro. 2g | **% daily value:** Vit. A 25%; Vit. C 0%; Calc. 6%; Iron 4% | **exchanges:** 1/2 Starch, 1/2 Fat | **CARB. CHOICES:** 1/2

Sun-Dried Tomato and Bacon Bruschetta

yum

2 Pt.

Total Carbs **9g**
Net Carbs **9g**

prep time:
35 minutes

start to finish:
50 minutes

24 slices (1/2 inch thick) baguette-style French bread (from 10-oz loaf)

1/2 cup julienne-cut sun-dried tomatoes packed in oil

1/2 cup chopped cooked bacon

3/4 cup finely shredded Fontina cheese (2 oz)

1/4 cup finely chopped fresh parsley

1 Heat oven to 400°F. In ungreased 15×10×1-inch pan, place bread slices.

2 In strainer over small bowl, place tomatoes; press tomatoes to drain oil into bowl (2 to 3 tablespoons oil is needed). Brush oil on bread. Bake 5 to 7 minutes or until crisp.

3 Top bread slices with tomatoes, bacon and cheese. Bake about 5 minutes or until cheese is melted. Sprinkle with parsley. Serve warm.

1 serving: Cal. 70 (Cal. from Fat 20); Fat 2.5g (Sat. fat 1g); Chol. 0mg; Sodium 150mg; Net Carbohydrate 9g; Carbs. 9g (Fiber 0g); Pro. 3g | **% daily value:** Vit. A 2%; Vit. C 2%; Calc. 2%; Iron 4% | **exchanges:** 1/2 Starch, 1/2 Fat | **CARB. CHOICES:** 1/2

Total Carbs **5g**
Net Carbs **5g**

prep time:
10 minutes

start to finish:
20 minutes

12 servings

yum!

Red Pepper Bruschetta

4 slices hard-crusted Italian or French bread, 1/2 inch thick

1 jar (7 oz) roasted red bell peppers, drained, cut into 1/2-inch strips

1 or 2 medium cloves garlic, finely chopped

2 tablespoons chopped fresh parsley or 1 teaspoon parsley flakes

2 tablespoons shredded Parmesan cheese

1 tablespoon olive or vegetable oil

1/4 teaspoon salt

1/4 teaspoon pepper

1 tablespoon capers, drained, if desired

1 Heat oven to 450°F. Place bread on ungreased cookie sheet. In small bowl, mix remaining ingredients except capers. Spoon onto bread.

2 Bake 6 to 8 minutes or until edges of bread are golden brown. Cut each slice lengthwise into thirds. Sprinkle with capers.

1 serving: Cal. 40 (Cal. from Fat 15); Fat 1.5g (Sat. fat 0g); Chol. 0mg; Sodium 110mg; Net Carbohydrate 5g; Carbs. 5g (Fiber 0g); Pro. 1g | **% daily value:** Vit. A 20%; Vit. C 25%; Calc. 2%; Iron 0% | **exchanges:** 1/2 Starch | **CARB. CHOICES:** 0

Red Pepper Bruschetta

Total Carbs **3g**
Net Carbs **3g**

prep time:
10 minutes

start to finish:
15 minutes

24 servings

Blue Cheese and Pear Triangles

1 Pt.
yuck

12 slices pumpernickel cocktail bread, cut diagonally in half

3 tablespoons mayonnaise or salad dressing

1 medium unpeeled red or green pear, thinly sliced and slices cut in half

2 tablespoons chopped drained roasted red bell peppers (from 7-oz jar)

1/3 cup crumbled blue cheese

1/3 cup chopped walnuts

Fresh marjoram leaves or chopped fresh chives, if desired

1 Heat oven to 400°F. Place bread on ungreased cookie sheet. Bake 4 to 5 minutes or until lightly toasted.

2 Spread mayonnaise over bread. Top with pear slices, bell pepper pieces, cheese, walnuts and marjoram. Serve immediately.

1 serving: Cal. 45 (Cal. from Fat 30); Fat 3g (Sat. fat 0.5g); Chol. 0mg; Sodium 60mg; Net Carbohydrate 3g; Carbs. 3g (Fiber 0g); Pro. 1g | **% daily value:** Vit. A 0%; Vit. C 4%; Calc. 0%; Iron 0% | **exchanges:** 1 Fat | **CARB. CHOICES:** 0

16 servings (2 tablespoons each)

Asiago Cheese and Artichoke Dip

yummy!
1 Pt.

Total Carbs **5g**
Net Carbs **4g**

prep time:
15 minutes

start to finish:
30 minutes

1 package (8 oz) fat-free cream cheese

1/2 cup fat-free sour cream

2 tablespoons fat-free half-and-half or evaporated fat-free milk

1/4 teaspoon salt

3/4 cup shredded Asiago cheese (3 oz)

1 can (14 oz) artichoke hearts, drained, chopped

4 medium green onions, chopped (1/4 cup)

2 tablespoons chopped fresh parsley

Crisp breadsticks or whole wheat crackers, if desired

1 Heat oven to 350°F. In medium bowl, beat cream cheese with electric mixer on medium speed until smooth. Beat in sour cream, half-and-half and salt. Stir in Asiago cheese, artichoke hearts and onions. Spoon into 1-quart casserole or small ovenproof serving dish.

2 Bake uncovered 10 to 15 minutes or until hot and cheese is melted. Remove from oven; stir. Sprinkle with parsley. Serve with breadsticks.

Microwave Directions: Use microwavable casserole or dish. Microwave uncovered on High 1 to 2 minutes, stirring every 30 seconds.

carb-bit

If you're cutting back on snacks like crackers, use steamed green beans and pieces of fresh red, orange and yellow bell peppers as dippers.

1 serving: Cal. 60 (Cal. from Fat 20); Fat 2.5g (Sat. fat 1.5g); Chol. 10mg; Sodium 250mg; Net Carbohydrate 4g; Carbs. 5g (Fiber 1g); Pro. 5g | **% daily value:** Vit. A 8%; Vit. C 6%; Calc. 10%; Iron 2% | **exchanges:** 1/2 Skim Milk, 1/2 Fat | **CARB. CHOICES:** 0

Total Carbs **4g**
Net Carbs **4g**

prep time:
20 minutes

start to finish:
35 minutes

Chipotle—Black Bean Dip

_1 pt_

yuck

2 large dried chipotle chilies

1 cup thick 'n chunky salsa

1/2 cup black bean dip (from 9-oz can)

2 tablespoons chopped fresh cilantro

1 cup shredded reduced-fat Cheddar or Colby-Monterey Jack cheese (4 oz)

2 medium green onions, chopped (2 tablespoons)

Sweet red cherry chili half, if desired

Reduced-fat tortilla chips, if desired

1 Heat oven to 350°F. Cover chilies with boiling water; let stand 10 minutes. Drain chilies and remove seeds. Chop chilies.

2 In medium bowl, mix chilies, salsa and bean dip. Stir in cilantro. Spoon into ungreased shallow 1-quart ovenproof serving dish. Sprinkle with cheese and onions.

3 Bake about 15 minutes or until mixture is hot and cheese is melted. Garnish with chili half. Serve with tortilla chips.

1 serving: Cal. 50 (Cal. from Fat 25); Fat 2.5g (Sat. fat 1.5g); Chol. 5mg; Sodium 200mg; Net Carbohydrate 4g; Carbs. 4g (Fiber 0g); Pro. 3g | **% daily value:** Vit. A 15%; Vit. C 2%; Calc. 6%; Iron 2% | **exchanges:** 1/2 High-Fat Meat | **CARB. CHOICES:** 0

2 Breakfast Favorites

Brunch Eggs on English Muffins   50

Potato-Basil Scramble   52

Vegetable Poached Eggs   53

Asian Omelet   54

Savory Italian Frittata   55

Spring Vegetable Frittata   56

Pizza Frittata   58

Impossibly Easy Ham and Swiss Pie   60

Cheesy Ham and Asparagus Bake   62

Green Chile, Egg and Potato Bake   63

Spicy Sausage Breakfast Squares   64

Honey Ham Bagel Sandwiches   66

Whole Wheat Waffles   68

= **super express** ready in 30 minutes or less

Total Carbs **19g**
Net Carbs **16g**

prep time:
25 minutes

start to finish:
25 minutes

4 servings

Brunch Eggs on English Muffins ok

Herbed Cheese Sauce

1 teaspoon butter or margarine

2 teaspoons all-purpose flour

1/2 cup fat-free (skim) milk

1/4 cup shredded reduced-fat Cheddar cheese (1 oz)

2 teaspoons grated reduced-fat Parmesan cheese blend

1/2 teaspoon chopped fresh or 1/4 teaspoon dried basil leaves

Dash of ground red pepper (cayenne)

Eggs

2 whole wheat English muffins, split

4 thin slices fully cooked Canadian-style bacon (2 oz)

2 cups fat-free cholesterol-free egg product

Freshly ground pepper

1 In 1-quart nonstick saucepan, melt butter over low heat. Stir in flour; remove from heat. Gradually stir in milk. Heat to boiling, stirring constantly. Boil and stir 1 minute; remove from heat. Stir in cheeses, basil and red pepper; keep warm.

2 Toast English muffins. In 10-inch nonstick skillet, cook bacon over medium heat until brown on both sides. Remove from skillet; keep warm.

3 Heat same skillet over medium heat. Pour egg product into skillet. As mixture begins to set at bottom and side, gently lift cooked portions with spatula so that thin, uncooked portion can flow to bottom. Avoid constant stirring. Cook 3 to 5 minutes or until thickened throughout but still moist.

4 Place 1 slice bacon on each muffin half. Top with eggs. Spoon about 2 tablespoons sauce over eggs. Sprinkle with pepper.

1 serving: Cal. 180 (Cal. from Fat 30); Fat 3.5g (Sat. fat 1.5g); Chol. 10mg; Sodium 730mg; Net Carbohydrate 16g; Carbs. 19g (Fiber 3g); Pro. 22g | **% daily value:** Vit. A 15%; Vit. C 0%; Calc. 20%; Iron 20% | **exchanges:** 1 Starch, 3 Very Lean Meat | **CARB. CHOICES:** 1

Brunch Eggs on English Muffins

prep time:
45 minutes

start to finish:
45 minutes

Try substituting bite-size pieces of cauliflower for the potatoes to reduce carbs.

4 servings

Potato-Basil Scramble
good - et good

2 medium white potatoes, peeled, cubed

1 medium onion, finely chopped (1/2 cup)

1 small red bell pepper, chopped (1/2 cup)

2 cups fat-free cholesterol-free egg product or 8 large eggs, beaten

2 tablespoons chopped fresh or 2 teaspoons dried basil leaves

1/2 teaspoon salt

1/8 teaspoon ground red pepper (cayenne)

1 In 2-quart saucepan, place potatoes. Add enough water just to cover potatoes. Heat to boiling; reduce heat to low. Cover and simmer 10 to 15 minutes or until tender; drain.

2 Spray 10-inch skillet with cooking spray. Cook potatoes, onion and bell pepper in skillet over medium heat about 5 minutes, stirring frequently, until hot.

3 In small bowl, mix remaining ingredients; pour into skillet. As mixture begins to set at bottom and side, gently lift cooked portions with spatula so that thin, uncooked portion can flow to bottom. Avoid constant stirring. Cook 3 to 5 minutes or until eggs are thickened throughout but still moist.

2 pt.

1 serving: Cal. 120 (Cal. from Fat 0); Fat 0g (Sat. fat 0g); Chol. 0mg; Sodium 530mg; Net Carbohydrate 15g; Carbs. 18g (Fiber 3g); Pro. 14g | **% daily value:** Vit. A 35%; Vit. C 35%; Calc. 6%; Iron 15% | **exchanges:** 1 Starch, 1 1/2 Very Lean Meat | **CARB. CHOICES:** 1

4 servings

Vegetable Poached Eggs

yuck

2 cups chopped broccoli

2 cups chopped fresh spinach (3 oz)

1 cup sliced fresh mushrooms (3 oz)

1 large onion, chopped (1 cup)

1 medium carrot, cut into julienne strips (1/2 cup)

1 small zucchini, cut into julienne strips (1/2 cup)

3/4 cup marinara sauce or spaghetti sauce

1/4 teaspoon pepper

4 large eggs

1/4 cup shredded mozzarella cheese (1 oz)

1 Spray 12-inch skillet with cooking spray; heat over medium heat. Cook broccoli, spinach, mushrooms, onion, carrot and zucchini in skillet 8 to 10 minutes, stirring occasionally, until vegetables are crisp-tender.

2 Stir in marinara sauce and pepper. Cook, stirring constantly, until hot.

3 Make four 3-inch indentations in vegetable mixture, using back of large spoon. Break 1 egg into each indentation. Cover and cook about 5 minutes or until egg whites and yolks are firm, not runny. Sprinkle with cheese. Serve immediately.

Total Carbs **19g**
Net Carbs **15g**

prep time:
15 minutes

start to finish:
35 minutes

carb-bit

Want fewer carbs? Save about 3 grams of carbs per serving by substituting 1 cup chopped cauliflower for the onion.

1 serving: Cal. 190 (Cal. from Fat 80); Fat 9g (Sat. fat 3g); Chol. 215mg; Sodium 370mg; Net Carbohydrate 15g; Carbs. 19g (Fiber 4g); Pro. 12g | **% daily value:** Vit. A 110%; Vit. C 45%; Calc. 15%; Iron 10% | **exchanges:** 1/2 Starch, 1/2 Other Carb., 1 Vegetable, 1 Medium-Fat Meat, 1/2 Fat | **CARB. CHOICES:** 1

Asian Omelet

Total Carbs **15g**
Net Carbs **13g**

prep time:
45 minutes

start to finish:
45 minutes

carb-bit

Both white and brown rice have about the same number of carbs cup for cup, but brown rice is higher in fiber. One cup of cooked white rice has less than 1 gram of fiber versus about 3 1/2 grams in a cup of brown rice.

6 large eggs

1/2 cup milk

1/2 teaspoon pepper

1 teaspoon vegetable oil

1 cup cooked brown or white rice

1 tablespoon finely chopped carrot

1 tablespoon finely chopped green bell pepper

1 tablespoon finely chopped red bell pepper

1 tablespoon finely chopped green onion

1 tablespoon finely chopped mushrooms

1 clove garlic, finely chopped

1 tablespoon soy sauce

1 In small bowl, beat eggs, milk and pepper slightly with fork or wire whisk; set aside. In 8-inch skillet or omelet pan, heat oil over medium-high heat. Cook remaining ingredients except soy sauce in oil, stirring frequently, until vegetables are crisp-tender. Stir in soy sauce. Remove mixture from skillet; keep warm.

2 Spray same skillet with cooking spray; heat over medium-high heat. Quickly pour about 1/2 cup of the egg mixture into skillet. Slide skillet back and forth rapidly over heat and, at the same time, quickly stir with fork to spread eggs continuously over bottom of skillet as they thicken. Let stand over heat a few seconds to lightly brown bottom of omelet. (Do not overcook—omelet will continue to cook after folding.)

3 Spoon about 1/4 cup of the rice mixture on one side of omelet. Run spatula under unfilled side of omelet; lift over rice mixture. Tilting skillet slightly, turn omelet onto plate. Repeat with remaining egg and rice mixtures.

1 serving: Cal. 190 (Cal. from Fat 90); Fat 10g (Sat. fat 3g); Chol. 320mg; Sodium 340mg; Net Carbohydrate 13g; Carbs. 15g (Fiber 2g); Pro. 12g | **% daily value:** Vit. A 20%; Vit. C 6%; Calc. 8%; Iron 8% | **exchanges:** 1 Starch, 1 Medium-Fat Meat, 1 Fat | **CARB. CHOICES:** 1

6 servings

Savory Italian Frittata

Total Carbs 2g
Net Carbs **2g**

prep time:
10 minutes

start to finish:
30 minutes

2 cups fat-free cholesterol-free egg product

1 tablespoon chopped fresh or 1/2 teaspoon dried basil leaves

1 tablespoon chopped fresh or 1/2 teaspoon dried mint leaves

1 tablespoon chopped fresh or 1/2 teaspoon dried sage leaves

1 tablespoon freshly grated Parmesan cheese

1/2 teaspoon salt

1/8 teaspoon pepper

1/4 cup diced fully cooked turkey ham or prosciutto (2 oz)

1 tablespoon butter or margarine

1 small onion, finely chopped (1/4 cup)

1 In medium bowl, beat all ingredients except turkey ham, butter and onion thoroughly with fork or wire whisk until well mixed. Stir in turkey ham.

2 In 10-inch nonstick skillet, melt butter over medium-high heat. Cook onion in butter 4 to 5 minutes, stirring frequently, until crisp-tender; reduce heat to medium-low.

3 Pour egg mixture into skillet. Cover and cook 9 to 11 minutes or until eggs are set around edge and light brown on bottom. Cut into wedges.

1 serving: Cal. 80 (Cal. from Fat 25); Fat 2.5g (Sat. fat 1.5g); Chol. 10mg; Sodium 480mg; Net Carbohydrate 2g; Carbs. 2g (Fiber 0g); Pro. 11g | **% daily value:** Vit. A 10%; Vit. C 0%; Calc. 4%; Iron 10% | **exchanges:** 1 1/2 Very Lean Meat, 1/2 Fat | **CARB. CHOICES:** 0

Total Carbs **6g**
Net Carbs **4g**

prep time:
15 minutes

start to finish:
30 minutes

6 servings

Spring Vegetable Frittata

2 tablespoons butter or margarine

1 medium onion, chopped (1/2 cup)

1 clove garlic, finely chopped

1 medium green or red bell pepper, chopped (1 cup)

2 small zucchini, chopped (2 cups)

1 small tomato, chopped (½ cup)

1/4 teaspoon salt

1/4 teaspoon pepper

1 1/2 cups fat-free cholesterol-free egg product

1/4 cup grated Parmesan cheese

1 Heat oven to 375°F.

2 In 10-inch ovenproof skillet, melt butter over medium-high heat. Cook onion and garlic in butter 3 minutes, stirring frequently. Stir in bell pepper; reduce heat to medium. Cook about 2 minutes, stirring occasionally, until crisp-tender. Stir in zucchini, tomato, salt and pepper. Cook 4 minutes, stirring occasionally. Stir in egg product.

3 Bake 10 to 12 minutes or until eggs are set in center. Sprinkle with cheese. Cut into wedges.

1 serving: Cal. 110 (Cal. from Fat 45); Fat 5g (Sat. fat 3g); Chol. 15mg; Sodium 320mg; Net Carbohydrate 4g; Carbs. 6g (Fiber 2g); Pro. 9g | **% daily value:** Vit. A 20%; Vit. C 25%; Calc. 10%; Iron 8% | **exchanges:** 1 Vegetable, 1 Very Lean Meat, 1 Fat | **CARB. CHOICES:** 1/2

Spring Vegetable Frittata

prep time:
20 minutes

start to finish:
30 minutes

5 servings

Pizza Frittata

2 cups fat-free cholesterol-free egg product

1/4 cup freshly grated Parmesan cheese

1 teaspoon Italian seasoning

1/4 teaspoon salt

1/4 teaspoon pepper

1 tablespoon butter or margarine

1 cup sliced fresh mushrooms (3 oz)

1 medium bell pepper, chopped (1 cup)

1 small onion, chopped (1/4 cup)

1/4 cup sliced ripe olives

1 In medium bowl, beat egg product, cheese, Italian seasoning, salt and pepper with fork or wire whisk until blended; set aside.

2 In ovenproof 12-inch nonstick skillet, melt butter over medium heat. Cook mushrooms, bell pepper, onion and olives in butter about 2 minutes, stirring occasionally, until vegetables are crisp-tender. Spread mixture evenly in bottom of skillet.

3 Pour egg mixture evenly over vegetable mixture; reduce heat to medium-low. Cover and cook 9 to 11 minutes or until eggs are set in center and light brown on bottom. Remove cover.

4 Set oven control to broil. Broil frittata with top about 5 inches from heat about 2 minutes or until golden brown. Cut into wedges.

1 serving: Cal. 110 (Cal. from Fat 40); Fat 4.5g (Sat. fat 2g); Chol. 10mg; Sodium 470mg; Net Carbohydrate 4g; Carbs. 6g (Fiber 2g); Pro. 13g | **% daily value:** Vit. A 15%; Vit. C 25%; Calc. 10%; Iron 15% | **exchanges:** 1/2 Starch, 1 1/2 Very Lean Meat, 1/2 Fat | **CARB. CHOICES:** 1/2

Pizza Frittata

Impossibly Easy Ham and Swiss Pie

1 cup cut-up fully cooked ham

1 cup shredded reduced-fat Swiss cheese (4 oz)

1/4 cup chopped green onions (4 medium) or other chopped onion

1/2 cup Original or Reduced Fat Bisquick® mix

1 cup fat-free (skim) milk

1/4 teaspoon salt, if desired

1/8 teaspoon pepper

2 large eggs

1 medium tomato, sliced

1 medium green bell pepper, cut into rings

1 Heat oven to 400°F. Spray 9-inch glass pie plate with cooking spray. Sprinkle ham, cheese and onions in pie plate.

2 In medium bowl, beat remaining ingredients except tomato and bell pepper with fork until blended. Pour into pie plate.

3 Bake 35 to 40 minutes or until knife inserted in center comes out clean. Let stand 5 minutes before cutting. Garnish with tomato and bell pepper.

Total Carbs **11g**
Net Carbs **11g**

prep time:
10 minutes

start to finish:
55 minutes

carb-bit

Fresh strawberries and blueberries are great fruit choices to go with this delicious breakfast bake.

---

1 serving: Cal. 160 (Cal. from Fat 60); Fat 6g (Sat. fat 2.5g); Chol. 90mg; Sodium 570mg; Net Carbohydrate 11g; Carbs. 11g (Fiber 0g); Pro. 15g | **% daily value:** Vit. A 10%; Vit. C 20%; Calc. 25%; Iron 6% | **exchanges:** 1/2 Starch, 2 Very Lean Meat, 1 Fat | **CARB. CHOICES:** 1

Impossibly Easy Ham and Swiss Pie

prep time:
15 minutes

start to finish:
45 minutes

8 servings

Cheesy Ham and Asparagus Bake

1 1/2 cups chopped fully cooked ham

1 medium onion, chopped (1/2 cup)

1/4 cup chopped bell pepper

1 box (9 oz) frozen asparagus cuts*

2 cups fat-free cholesterol-free egg product

2 cups fat-free (skim) milk

1 cup all-purpose flour

1/4 cup grated **Parmesan** cheese

3/4 teaspoon salt

3/4 teaspoon dried tarragon leaves**

1/2 teaspoon pepper

1 cup shredded reduced-fat **Cheddar** cheese (4 oz)

1 Heat oven to 425°F. Spray 13×9-inch glass baking dish with cooking spray. Sprinkle ham, onion, bell pepper and asparagus in baking dish.

2 In large bowl, mix egg product, milk, flour, Parmesan cheese, salt, tarragon and pepper with fork or wire whisk until smooth; pour over ham mixture.

3 Bake uncovered about 20 minutes or until knife inserted in center comes out clean. Sprinkle with Cheddar cheese. Bake 3 to 5 minutes longer or until cheese is melted. Let stand 5 minutes before cutting.

*1 box (9 oz) frozen broccoli cuts can be substituted for the asparagus.

**Dried basil leaves can be substituted for the tarragon.

1 serving: Cal. 200 (Cal. from Fat 40); Fat 4.5g (Sat. fat 2g); Chol. 20mg; Sodium 940mg; Net Carbohydrate 17g; Carbs. 19g (Fiber 2g); Pro. 22g | **% daily value:** Vit. A 15%; Vit. C 10%; Calc. 25%; Iron 15% | **exchanges:** 1 1/2 Starch, 2 1/2 Very Lean Meat | **CARB. CHOICES:** 1

Green Chile, Egg and Potato Bake

Total Carbs **18g**
Net Carbs **15g**

prep time:
15 minutes

start to finish:
**1 hour
25 minutes**

2 1/2 cups frozen diced hash brown potatoes, thawed

1/4 cup frozen whole kernel corn (from 1-lb bag), thawed

1/4 cup chopped drained roasted red bell peppers (from 7-oz jar)

1 can (4.5 oz) chopped green chiles, drained

1 1/2 cups shredded reduced-fat Cheddar cheese (6 oz)

2 1/2 cups fat-free cholesterol-free egg product

1/2 cup fat-free small curd cottage cheese

1/2 teaspoon dried oregano leaves

1/4 teaspoon garlic powder

4 medium green onions, chopped (1/4 cup)

1 Heat oven to 350°F. Spray 11×7-inch glass baking dish with cooking spray. Layer potatoes, corn, bell peppers, chiles and 1 cup of the Cheddar cheese in baking dish.

2 In medium bowl, beat egg product, cottage cheese, oregano and garlic powder with electric mixer on medium speed until smooth. Slowly pour over mixture in dish. Sprinkle with onions and remaining 1/2 cup cheese.

3 Cover with foil and bake 30 minutes. Uncover and bake about 30 minutes longer or until top is golden brown and center is set. Let stand 10 minutes before cutting.

1 serving: Cal. 150 (Cal. from Fat 15); Fat 2g (Sat. fat 1g); Chol. 0mg; Sodium 810mg; Net Carbohydrate 15g; Carbs. 18g (Fiber 3g); Pro. 16g | **% daily value:** Vit. A 20%; Vit. C 15%; Calc. 20%; Iron 10% | **exchanges:** 1 Starch, 2 Very Lean Meat | **CARB. CHOICES:** 1

Spicy Sausage Breakfast Squares

Total Carbs **15g**
Net Carbs **15g**

prep time:
30 minutes

start to finish:
55 minutes

carb-bit

Arrange alternating slices of orange and kiwifruit on a serving platter. Not only will the fruits add color, they'll also help cool the spiciness of these breakfast squares.

1 package (12 oz) frozen bulk hot pork sausage, thawed

1/3 cup chopped onion

2 cloves garlic, finely chopped

1 medium red bell pepper, chopped (1 cup)

1 1/2 cups all-purpose flour

1/4 teaspoon salt

1/4 teaspoon crushed red pepper flakes

1 cup milk

3 large eggs

1 1/2 cups shredded Mexican cheese blend (6 oz)

1 Heat oven to 425°F. Spray 13×9-inch pan with cooking spray. In 12-inch skillet, cook sausage, onion and garlic over medium heat, stirring frequently, until sausage is no longer pink; drain. Stir in bell pepper; remove from heat.

2 In large bowl, beat flour, salt, red pepper flakes, milk and eggs with wire whisk until smooth. Pour into pan. Spoon pork mixture over batter. Sprinkle with cheese.

3 Bake uncovered 22 to 27 minutes or until top is golden brown.

1 serving: Cal. 190 (Cal. from Fat 90); Fat 10g (Sat. fat 5g); Chol. 80mg; Sodium 340mg; Net Carbohydrate 15g; Carbs. 15g (Fiber 0g); Pro. 10g | **% daily value:** Vit. A 20%; Vit. C 20%; Calc. 15%; Iron 6% | **exchanges:** 1 Starch, 1 High-Fat Meat | **CARB. CHOICES:** 1

Spicy Sausage Breakfast Squares

prep time:
15 minutes

start to finish:
15 minutes

4 open-face sandwiches

Honey Ham Bagel Sandwiches

2 pumpernickel or whole wheat bagels, split, toasted

4 teaspoons honey mustard

4 slices (1 oz each) fully cooked honey baked ham

4 thin slices (1/2 oz each) Swiss cheese

1 Heat oven to 400°F. Spread each bagel half with 1 teaspoon mustard. Top each with ham and cheese. Place on cookie sheet.

2 Bake 3 to 5 minutes or until cheese is melted.

1 sandwich: Cal. 180 (Cal. from Fat 60); Fat 7g (Sat. fat 3.5g); Chol. 30mg; Sodium 610mg; Net Carbohydrate 16g; Carbs. 18g (Fiber 2g); Pro. 13g | **% daily value:** Vit. A 2%; Vit. C 0%; Calc. 15%; Iron 8% | **exchanges:** 1 Starch, 1 1/2 Medium-Fat Meat | **CARB. CHOICES:** 1

Honey Ham Bagel Sandwiches

prep time:
10 minutes

start to finish:
25 minutes

carb-bit

At 25 calories per tablespoon, wheat germ is a concentrated source of vitamins, minerals and protein. Serve these nutty-flavored waffles with unsweetened applesauce or sugar-free jam or jelly.

12 servings

Whole Wheat Waffles

1/2 cup fat-free cholesterol-free egg product or 2 large eggs

2 cups whole wheat flour

1/4 cup butter or margarine, melted

1 3/4 cups fat-free (skim) milk

1 tablespoon sugar

3 teaspoons baking powder

1/2 teaspoon salt

6 tablespoons wheat germ

1 Spray waffle iron with cooking spray; heat waffle iron. In medium bowl, beat egg product with hand beater until fluffy. Beat in remaining ingredients except wheat germ just until smooth.

2 For each waffle, pour about one-third of batter onto center of hot waffle iron; sprinkle with 2 tablespoons wheat germ. Bake about 5 minutes or until steaming stops. Carefully remove waffle. Separate each waffle into fourths.

1 serving: Cal. 130 (Cal. from Fat 40); Fat 4.5g (Sat. fat 2g); Chol. 10mg; Sodium 280mg; Net Carbohydrate 16g; Carbs. 19g (Fiber 3g); Pro. 6g | **% daily value:** Vit. A 6%; Vit. C 0%; Calc. 10%; Iron 8% | **exchanges:** 1 Starch, 1/2 Very Lean Meat, 1 Fat | **CARB. CHOICES:** 1

3 Simply Meat

Gingered Flank Steak   72

Broiled Herb Steak   73

Italian Steak and Vegetables   74

Steakhouse Sirloin au Jus   76

Beef with Spiced Pepper Sauce   77

Sirloin with Bacon-Dijon Sauce   78

Swiss Steak   79

Spicy Pepper Steak   80

Hearty Beef and Vegetables   81

Savory Beef Tenderloin   82

Three-Pepper Beef Tenderloin   83

Broiled Dijon Burgers   84

Giant Oven Burger   86

Meat Loaf   87

Beef Stew, Bologna Style   88

Veal with Asparagus   90

Breaded Pork Chops   92

Southwestern Pork Chops   94

Honey-Mustard Pork Chops   96

Greek Honey and Lemon
    Pork Chops   97

Pork Medallions with
    Hot Pineapple Glaze   98

Garlicky Pork with Basil   99

Pork with Rich Vegetable Gravy   100

Caramelized Pork Slices   101

Caribbean Pork Tenderloin   102

Italian Roasted Pork Tenderloin   104

Mustard Lamb Chops   105

Lamb with Creamy Mint Sauce   106

◑ = **super express** ready in 30 minutes or less

Variety—It's the Spice of Life!

Bring a world of flavor variety to your tired taste buds! Explore and savor, from simple to fancy, mild to bold, familiar to exotic. So move over, salt and pepper, because a flavor explosion is moving in on your turf. Whether your beef, pork, chicken, fish or seafood is bathed in marinade or slathered with an intense rub, it's going to be good. Give one of these great flavor boosters a try—they're easy and delicious.

1 For marinades

Make marinade as directed. Combine beef, pork, chicken, fish or seafood and marinade in a resealable plastic food-storage bag or shallow glass or plastic container. Seal bag or cover container and refrigerate beef, pork or chicken at least 4 hours but no longer than 24 hours. Refrigerate fish and seafood up to 30 minutes; longer marinating time may cause the texture to become soft and mushy. However, firm-fleshed fish like halibut, swordfish and tuna can be refrigerated up to 4 hours. Remove from marinade and cook as desired.

2 For rubs

Make rub as directed, and cook food as desired.

3 Enjoy!

Barbecue Sauce

1 cup ketchup	1/4 teaspoon pepper
1/4 cup butter or margarine	1 medium onion, finely chopped (1/2 cup)
1/3 cup water	
1 tablespoon paprika	2 tablespoons lemon juice
1 teaspoon packed brown sugar	1 tablespoon Worcestershire sauce

In 1 1/2-quart saucepan, heat all ingredients except lemon juice and Worcestershire sauce to boiling over medium heat. Stir in lemon juice and Worcestershire sauce. Heat until hot. Bake, broil or grill beef, pork or chicken. For broiling or grilling, brush on sauce during last 10 to 15 minutes of cooking. About 2 cups sauce.

2 tablespoons: Cal. 50 (Cal. from Fat 25); Fat 3g (Sat. fat 1.5g); Chol. 10mg; Sodium 210mg; Carbs. 5g (Fiber 0g); Pro. 0g | **% daily value:** Vit. A 10%; Vit. C 2%; Calc. 0%; Iron 0% | **exchanges:** 1/2 Other Carb. | **CARB. CHOICES:** 0

Garlic Marinade

2 tablespoons olive or vegetable oil

4 cloves garlic, finely chopped

1 tablespoon chopped fresh or 1 teaspoon dried rosemary leaves, crumbled

1/2 teaspoon ground mustard

1 tablespoon water

2 teaspoons soy sauce

3 tablespoons red or white wine vinegar, dry sherry or apple juice

In 10-inch nonstick skillet, heat oil over medium-high heat. Cook garlic in oil, stirring frequently, until golden. Stir in rosemary, mustard, water and soy sauce; remove from heat. Stir in vinegar; cool. Use to marinate 1 pound beef, pork or chicken. Bake, broil or grill meat. About 1/2 cup marinade.

1 tablespoon: Cal. 35 (Cal. from Fat 30); Fat 3.5g (Sat. fat 0g); Chol. 0mg; Sodium 75mg; Carbs. 1g (Fiber 0g); Pro. 0g | **% daily value:** Vit. A 0%; Vit. C 0%; Calc. 0%; Iron 0% | **exchanges:** 1/2 Fat | **CARB. CHOICES:** 0

Citrus Marinade

1 tablespoon chopped fresh or 1 teaspoon dried basil leaves

3 tablespoons orange juice

2 tablespoons lemon juice

2 tablespoons olive or vegetable oil

1/2 teaspoon salt

1/4 teaspoon pepper

2 cloves garlic, finely chopped

In small bowl, mix all ingredients. Use to marinate 1 pound pork, chicken or fish. Bake, broil or grill meat. About 1/2 cup marinade.

1 tablespoon: Cal. 35 (Cal. from Fat 30); Fat 3.5g (Sat. fat 0g); Chol. 0mg; Sodium 150mg; Carbs. 1g (Fiber 0g); Pro. 0g | **% daily value:** Vit. A 0%; Vit. C 2%; Calc. 0%; Iron 0% | **exchanges:** 1/2 Fat | **CARB. CHOICES:** 0

Herb Rub

2 teaspoons olive or vegetable oil

1 tablespoon dried tarragon leaves

2 teaspoons dried thyme leaves

1 1/2 teaspoons dried sage leaves, crumbled

1/2 teaspoon onion powder

1/4 teaspoon salt

Rub oil on 1 pound beef, pork or chicken. In small bowl, mix remaining ingredients; rub on meat. Bake, broil or grill meat. About 2 tablespoons rub.

1 1/2 teaspoons: Cal. 30 (Cal. from Fat 20); Fat 2.5g (Sat. fat 0g); Chol. 0mg; Sodium 150mg; Carbs. 1g (Fiber 0g); Pro. 0g | **% daily value:** Vit. A 0%; Vit. C 0%; Calc. 2%; Iron 6% | **exchanges:** 1/2 Fat | **CARB. CHOICES:** 0

Gingered Flank Steak

I lb beef flank steak

1/3 cup lemon juice

2 tablespoons honey

I tablespoon reduced-sodium soy sauce

2 teaspoons grated gingerroot or
I teaspoon ground ginger

2 cloves garlic, finely chopped

1 Trim fat from beef. Make cuts in both sides of beef about 1/2 inch apart and 1/8 inch deep in diamond pattern. In shallow glass or plastic dish, mix remaining ingredients. Place beef in dish; turn to coat both sides. Cover and refrigerate at least 8 hours but no longer than 24 hours, turning beef occasionally.

2 Set oven control to broil. Remove beef from marinade; reserve marinade. Spray broiler pan rack with cooking spray. Place beef on rack in broiler pan. Broil with top about 3 inches from heat about 12 minutes for medium (160°F), turning after 6 minutes and brushing frequently with marinade. Discard any remaining marinade. Cut beef across grain at slanted angle into thin slices.

Total Carbs 11g
Net Carbs 11g

prep time:
20 minutes

start to finish:
**8 hours
20 minutes**

carb-bit

Take a carb break—serve with strips of sautéed zucchini, yellow summer squash and red bell pepper instead of the traditional high-carb rice or noodles.

I serving: Cal. 220 (Cal. from Fat 70); Fat 8g (Sat. fat 3g); Chol. 65mg; Sodium 200mg; Net Carbohydrate 11g; Carbs. 11g (Fiber 0g); Pro. 25g | **% daily value:** Vit. A 0%; Vit. C 4%; Calc. 0%; Iron 15% | **exchanges:** 1/2 Other Carb., 3 1/2 Lean Meat | **CARB. CHOICES:** I

8 servings

Broiled Herb Steak

2 lb beef bone-in top round steak, about 1 inch thick

1 tablespoon chopped fresh or 1 teaspoon dried basil leaves

2 tablespoons reduced-sodium soy sauce

1 tablespoon vegetable oil

1 tablespoon ketchup

2 teaspoons chopped fresh or 1/2 teaspoon dried oregano leaves

1/2 teaspoon salt

1/2 teaspoon coarsely ground pepper

1 clove garlic, finely chopped

Total Carbs **1g**
Net Carbs **1g**

prep time:
30 minutes

start to finish:
**5 hours
30 minutes**

1 Remove fat from beef. Place beef on large piece of plastic wrap. In small bowl, mix remaining ingredients; brush on both sides of beef. Fold plastic wrap over beef and secure tightly. Refrigerate at least 5 hours but no longer than 24 hours.

2 Set oven control to broil. Place beef on rack in broiler pan. Broil with top about 3 inches from heat 16 to 20 minutes for medium (160°F), turning after 8 minutes. Cut beef across grain at slanted angle into 1/4-inch slices.

1 serving: Cal. 140 (Cal. from Fat 45); Fat 5g (Sat. fat 1.5g); Chol. 60mg; Sodium 350mg; Net Carbohydrate 1g; Carbs. 1g (Fiber 0g); Pro. 23g | **% daily value:** Vit. A 2%; Vit. C 0%; Calc. 0%; Iron 10% | **exchanges:** 3 1/2 Very Lean Meat, 1/2 Fat | **CARB. CHOICES:** 0

Total Carbs **7g**
Net Carbs **9g**

prep time:
25 minutes

start to finish:
40 minutes

Italian Steak and Vegetables

1/2 cup balsamic vinaigrette dressing

1/4 cup chopped fresh basil leaves

1 1/2 teaspoons peppered seasoned salt

2 beef boneless New York strip steaks, about 1 inch thick (8 to 10 oz each)

1 lb asparagus spears, cut into 2-inch pieces

1 medium red onion, cut into thin wedges

1 yellow bell pepper, cut into 8 pieces

1 In large bowl, mix 2 tablespoons of the dressing, 2 tablespoons of the basil and 3/4 teaspoon of the peppered seasoned salt; set aside for vegetables. In shallow glass or plastic dish or resealable plastic food-storage bag, mix remaining dressing, basil and peppered seasoned salt; add beef. Cover dish or seal bag and refrigerate 15 minutes.

2 Heat coals or gas grill for direct heat. Add asparagus, onion and bell pepper to reserved dressing mixture; toss to coat. Place in disposable 8-inch square foil pan or grill basket (grill "wok"). Reserve dressing in bowl.

3 Remove beef from marinade; reserve marinade. Cover and grill pan of vegetables over medium heat 5 minutes. Add beef to grill next to pan. Cover and grill beef and vegetables 10 to 12 minutes, turning beef once and stirring vegetables occasionally, until beef is desired doneness and vegetables are tender. Brush beef with reserved marinade during last 5 minutes of grilling.

4 Add vegetables to bowl with reserved dressing; toss to coat. Cut beef into thin slices. Discard any remaining marinade. Serve vegetables with beef. Drizzle with additional dressing if desired.

1 serving: Cal. 240 (Cal. from Fat 80); Fat 9g (Sat. fat 3.5g); Chol. 75mg; Sodium 580mg; Net Carbohydrate 7g; Carbs. 9g (Fiber 2g); Pro. 30g | **% daily value:** Vit. A 20%; Vit. C 60%; Calc. 4%; Iron 20% | **exchanges:** 1 1/2 Vegetable, 4 Very Lean Meat, 1 1/2 Fat | **CARB. CHOICES:** 1/2

Italian Steak and Vegetables

Total Carbs **2g**
Net Carbs **2g**

prep time:
25 minutes

start to finish:
25 minutes

carb-bit

Instead of serving potatoes, try cooking cauliflower pieces with a clove of garlic just until tender; drain. In a food processor, process the cauliflower and garlic with a little olive oil, butter or low-fat mayonnaise and salt to taste, until desired consistency—they will be remarkably similar to mashed potatoes. And, cauliflower has 2 grams of carbs per half cup compared to 11.6 grams in half of one small baked potato.

4 servings

Steakhouse Sirloin au Jus

1 1/4 cups fat-free beef broth

1 tablespoon Worcestershire sauce

1 tablespoon balsamic or red wine vinegar

1/2 teaspoon sugar

2 cloves garlic, finely chopped

1 lb beef boneless sirloin steak, about 3/4 inch thick

1/4 cup chopped fresh parsley

Freshly ground pepper

1   In small bowl, beat broth, Worcestershire sauce, vinegar, sugar and garlic with wire whisk until blended; set aside.

2   Spray 10-inch skillet with cooking spray; heat over medium-high heat. Cook beef in skillet 8 to 10 minutes, turning once, until brown. Remove beef from skillet; keep warm.

3   Add broth mixture to skillet; heat to boiling. Boil 5 minutes, stirring constantly, until sauce is reduced to 1/3 cup; remove from heat.

4   Cut beef across grain at slanted angle into thin slices. Serve sauce over beef. Sprinkle with parsley and pepper.

1 serving: Cal. 130 (Cal. from Fat 30); Fat 3.5g (Sat. fat 1g); Chol. 60mg; Sodium 240mg; Net Carbohydrate 2g; Carbs. 2g (Fiber 0g); Pro. 23g | **% daily value:** Vit. A 8%; Vit. C 6%; Calc. 0%; Iron 15% | **exchanges:** 3 Lean Meat | **CARB. CHOICES:** 0

4 servings

Beef with Spiced Pepper Sauce

Total Carbs 6g
Net Carbs 6g

prep time:
30 minutes

start to finish:
30 minutes

1 lb beef top sirloin steak, about 3/4 inch thick

3 tablespoons ketchup

3 tablespoons water

3/4 teaspoon soy sauce

1/2 medium green bell pepper, cut into thin strips

1 small onion, thinly sliced

Coarsely ground pepper

1 Remove fat from beef. Between pieces of plastic wrap or waxed paper, place beef; pound with meat mallet or rolling pin to tenderize. Cut beef into 4 serving pieces.

2 In small bowl, beat ketchup, water and soy sauce with wire whisk until blended; set aside.

3 Spray 10-inch skillet with cooking spray; heat over medium-high heat. Cook beef in skillet 3 minutes, turning once. Add bell pepper and onion. Stir in ketchup mixture; reduce heat to low. Cover and simmer 12 minutes. Remove beef from skillet; keep warm.

4 Stir ground pepper into sauce in skillet; heat to boiling. Boil 2 minutes, stirring frequently, until sauce is slightly thickened. Serve sauce over beef.

1 serving: Cal. 150 (Cal. from Fat 30); Fat 3.5g (Sat. fat 1g); Chol. 60mg; Sodium 230mg; Net Carbohydrate 6g; Carbs. 6g (Fiber 0g); Pro. 23g | **% daily value:** Vit. A 6%; Vit. C 15%; Calc. 0%; Iron 15% | **exchanges:** 1/2 Other Carb., 3 Very Lean Meat, 1/2 Fat | **CARB. CHOICES:** 1/2

Total Carbs 0g
Net Carbs 0g

prep time:
25 minutes

start to finish:
25 minutes

carb-bit

Unsweetened varieties of mustard contain negligible carbs. You'll find many kinds in your grocery store and even more in gourmet and kitchen specialty shops. Choose your favorite, or experiment with different kinds to vary the flavor of this great-tasting beef.

4 servings

Sirloin with Bacon-Dijon Sauce

4 slices bacon, cut into ½-inch pieces

I lb beef boneless sirloin steak, ¾ inch thick

1/2 teaspoon peppered seasoned salt

1/2 cup beef broth

2 teaspoons Dijon mustard

1/2 teaspoon chopped fresh or 1/8 teaspoon dried thyme leaves

4 medium green onions, sliced (1/4 cup)

1　In 12-inch nonstick skillet, cook bacon over medium heat, stirring occasionally, until crisp. Remove bacon from skillet with slotted spoon; drain on paper towels. Reserve 1 tablespoon bacon fat in skillet.

2　Cut beef into 4 serving pieces. Sprinkle with peppered seasoned salt. Cook beef in bacon fat in skillet over medium heat about 6 minutes, turning once, until desired doneness. Remove beef from skillet; keep warm.

3　In skillet, mix broth, mustard, thyme and onions. Cook over medium heat, stirring occasionally, until slightly thickened. Serve sauce over beef. Sprinkle with bacon.

I serving: Cal. 180 (Cal. from Fat 70); Fat 8g (Sat. fat 2.5g); Chol. 65mg; Sodium 530mg; Net Carbohydrate 0g; Carbs. 0g (Fiber 0g); Pro. 26g | **% daily value:** Vit. A 2%; Vit. C 0%; Calc. 0%; Iron 15% | **exchanges:** 3 1/2 Lean Meat | **CARB. CHOICES:** 0

6 servings

Swiss Steak

1 1/2 lb beef boneless round, tip or chuck steak, about 3/4 inch thick

3 tablespoons all-purpose flour

1 teaspoon ground mustard

1/2 teaspoon salt

2 teaspoons vegetable oil

1 can (14.5 oz) whole tomatoes, undrained

2 cloves garlic, finely chopped

1 cup water

1 large onion, sliced

1 large green bell pepper, sliced

Total Carbs **10g**
Net Carbs **8g**

prep time:
40 minutes

start to finish:
**1 hour
55 minutes**

1 Remove fat from beef. In small bowl, mix flour, mustard and salt. Sprinkle half of the flour mixture over one side of beef; pound in. Turn beef; pound in remaining flour mixture. Cut beef into 6 serving pieces.

2 In 10-inch nonstick skillet, heat oil over medium heat. Cook beef in oil about 15 minutes, turning once, until brown. Stir in tomatoes and garlic, breaking up tomatoes. Heat to boiling; reduce heat to low. Cover and simmer about 1 hour 15 minutes or until beef is tender.

3 Stir in water, onion and bell pepper. Heat to boiling; reduce heat to low. Cover and simmer 5 to 8 minutes or until vegetables are tender.

1 serving: Cal. 180 (Cal. from Fat 50); Fat 5g (Sat. fat 1.5g); Chol. 60mg; Sodium 340mg; Net Carbohydrate 8g; Carbs. 10g (Fiber 2g); Pro. 24g | **% daily value:** Vit. A 8%; Vit. C 30%; Calc. 4%; Iron 15% | **exchanges:** 1/2 Other Carb., 3 1/2 Very Lean Meat, 1/2 Fat | **CARB. CHOICES:** 1/2

Total Carbs 11g
Net Carbs 9g

prep time:
15 minutes

start to finish:
15 minutes

carb-bit

A mixture of soy-beans, garlic and chili peppers, hoisin sauce is fat free with about 15 grams of carb for 2 tablespoons. Its greatest attribute is that it's loaded with flavor—a little goes a long way!

4 servings

Spicy Pepper Steak

I tablespoon chili oil or vegetable oil
I lb cut-up beef for stir-fry
I large bell pepper, cut into 3/4-inch squares

I medium onion, sliced
1/4 cup hoisin sauce

1 In 12-inch nonstick skillet, heat oil over medium-high heat. Add beef; cook and stir about 2 minutes or until brown.

2 Add bell pepper and onion; cook and stir about 1 minute or until vegetables are crisp-tender. Stir in hoisin sauce; cook and stir about 30 seconds or until hot.

I serving: Cal. 210 (Cal. from Fat 70); Fat 8g (Sat. fat 2g); Chol. 60mg; Sodium 300mg; Net Carbohydrate 9g; Carbs. 11g (Fiber 2g); Pro. 24g | **% daily value:** Vit. A 10%; Vit. C 35%; Calc. 2%; Iron 15% | **exchanges:** 1/2 Other Carb., 3 1/2 Lean Meat | **CARB. CHOICES:** 1

4 servings

Hearty Beef and Vegetables

1 lb beef top sirloin steak, about 3/4 inch thick

1 bag (12 oz) frozen stew vegetables, thawed and drained

1 cup frozen cut green beans (from 1-lb bag), thawed, drained

1/2 cup water

1 tablespoon Worcestershire sauce

1 package (1 oz) onion soup mix (from 2-oz box)

3 tablespoons chopped fresh parsley

Total Carbs **13g**
Net Carbs **11g**

prep time:
30 minutes

start to finish:
30 minutes

1 Remove fat from beef. Cut beef into 1/2-inch pieces. Spray 4-quart Dutch oven with cooking spray; heat over medium-high heat. Cook beef in Dutch oven 2 minutes, stirring constantly.

2 Stir in stew vegetables, green beans, water, Worcestershire sauce and soup mix (dry). Heat to boiling; reduce heat to low. Cover and simmer 12 to 14 minutes, stirring occasionally, until potatoes are just tender; remove from heat. Stir in parsley.

1 serving: Cal. 180 (Cal. from Fat 30); Fat 3.5g (Sat. fat 1g); Chol. 60mg; Sodium 730mg; Net Carbohydrate 11g; Carbs. 13g (Fiber 2g); Pro. 24g | **% daily dalue:** Vit. A 10%; Vit. C 8%; Calc. 4%; Iron 15% | **exchanges:** 1/2 Starch, 1 Vegetable, 3 Very Lean Meat, 1/2 Fat | **CARB. CHOICES:** 1

super *express*

Total Carbs **7g**
Net Carbs **7g**

prep time:
25 minutes

start to finish:
25 minutes

4 servings

Savory Beef Tenderloin

3/4 lb beef tenderloin

**2 teaspoons chopped fresh or
1/2 teaspoon dried marjoram leaves**

2 teaspoons sugar

I teaspoon coarsely ground pepper

I tablespoon butter or margarine

I cup sliced fresh mushrooms (3 oz)

I small onion, thinly sliced

3/4 cup beef broth

**1/4 cup dry red wine or nonalcoholic
wine**

I tablespoon cornstarch

1 Cut beef into four 3/4-inch-thick slices. Mix marjoram, sugar and pepper; rub on both sides of beef slices. In 10-inch skillet, melt butter over medium heat. Cook beef in butter 3 to 5 minutes, turning once, until brown. Remove beef to serving platter; keep warm.

2 Cook mushrooms and onion in drippings in skillet over medium heat about 2 minutes, stirring occasionally, until onion is crisp-tender.

3 In small bowl, mix broth, wine and cornstarch; stir into mushroom mixture. Cook over medium heat, stirring constantly, until mixture thickens and boils. Boil and stir 1 minute. Pour over beef.

I serving: Cal. 220 (Cal. from Fat 120); Fat 13g (Sat. fat 5g); Chol. 60mg; Sodium 260mg; Net Carbohydrate 7g; Carbs. 7g (Fiber 0g); Pro. 19g | **% daily value:** Vit. A 4%; Vit. C 0%; Calc. 0%; Iron 15% | **exchanges:** 1/2 Starch, 2 1/2 Lean Meat, I Fat | **CARB. CHOICES:** 1/2

6 servings

Three-Pepper Beef Tenderloin

1 tablespoon freshly ground black pepper

2 teaspoons white pepper

2 teaspoons fennel seed, crushed

1/2 teaspoon salt

1/2 teaspoon ground thyme

1/4 teaspoon ground red pepper (cayenne)

1 1/2 lb beef tenderloin

1 In small bowl, mix all ingredients except beef; rub over beef. Cover and refrigerate at least 2 hours but no longer than 24 hours.

2 Heat oven to 350°F. Spray shallow roasting pan with cooking spray. Place beef in pan. Insert meat thermometer so tip is in center of thickest part of beef. Bake uncovered about 40 minutes or until thermometer reads 140°F (medium-rare doneness). Cover beef loosely with tent of foil and let stand about 15 minutes. (Temperature will continue to rise about 5°F, and beef will be easier to carve as juices set up.) Cut beef across grain at slanted angle into thin slices.

Total Carbs **2g**
Net Carbs **2g**

prep time:
10 minutes

start to finish:
**3 hours
5 minutes**

carb-bit

This spicy peppered steak is not for timid taste buds! Serve with a crisp green salad and steamed green beans to help balance the spiciness.

1 serving: Cal. 180 (Cal. from Fat 70); Fat 8g (Sat. fat 3g); Chol. 65mg; Sodium 260mg; Net Carbohydrate 2g; Carbs. 2g (Fiber 0g); Pro. 25g | **% daily value:** Vit. A 2%; Vit. C 0%; Calc. 2%; Iron 15% | **exchanges:** 3 1/2 Lean Meat | **CARB. CHOICES:** 0

prep time:
20 minutes

start to finish:
20 minutes

6 servings

Broiled Dijon Burgers

1/4 cup fat-free cholesterol-free egg product or 2 large egg whites

2 tablespoons fat-free (skim) milk

2 teaspoons Dijon mustard

1/4 teaspoon salt

1/8 teaspoon pepper

1 cup soft bread crumbs (about 2 slices bread)

1 small onion, finely chopped (1/4 cup)

1 lb extra-lean (at least 90%) ground beef

Hamburger buns, split and toasted, if desired

1 Set oven control to broil. Spray broiler pan rack with cooking spray.

2 In large bowl, mix egg product, milk, mustard, salt and pepper. Stir in bread crumbs and onion. Stir in beef. Shape mixture into 6 patties, each about 1/2 inch thick. Place patties on rack in broiler pan.

3 Broil with tops about 5 inches from heat about 10 minutes for medium, turning once, until no longer pink in center and meat thermometer inserted in center reads 160°F. Serve patties on buns.

1 serving: Cal. 190 (Cal. from Fat 60); Fat 7g (Sat. fat 2.5g); Chol. 45mg; Sodium 350mg; Net Carbohydrate 14g; Carbs. 14g (Fiber 0g); Pro. 18g | **% daily value:** Vit. A 2%; Vit. C 0%; Calc. 6%; Iron 15% | **exchanges:** 1 Starch, 2 Lean Meat | **CARB. CHOICES:** 1

Broiled Dijon Burgers

Giant Oven Burger

Total Carbs **5g**
Net Carbs **4g**

prep time:
10 minutes

start to finish:
**1 hour
5 minutes**

1 lb extra-lean (at least 90%) ground beef

1 small bell pepper, finely chopped (1/2 cup)

1 small onion, finely chopped (1/4 cup)

1 tablespoon prepared horseradish

1 tablespoon yellow mustard

1/2 teaspoon salt

1/3 cup chili sauce or ketchup

1 Heat oven to 350°F. In large bowl, mix all ingredients except chili sauce. In ungreased 9-inch glass pie plate, press beef mixture. Spread chili sauce over top.

2 Bake uncovered 45 to 50 minutes or until no longer pink in center and meat thermometer inserted in center reads 160°F; drain. Let stand 5 minutes. Cut into wedges.

carb-bit

Instead of bread serve the burger wedges between crispy iceberg lettuce leaves. Lots of crunch—no carbs!

1 serving: Cal. 130 (Cal. from Fat 60); Fat 6g (Sat. fat 2.5g); Chol. 45mg; Sodium 470mg; Net Carbohydrate 4g; Carbs. 5g (Fiber 1g); Pro. 15g | **% daily value:** Vit. A 4%; Vit. C 10%; Calc. 0%; Iron 10% | **exchanges:** 1/2 Other Carb., 2 Lean Meat | **CARB. CHOICES:** 0

Meat Loaf

Total Carbs **6g**
Net Carbs **5g**

3/4 lb extra-lean (at least 90%) ground beef

3/4 lb ground turkey breast

1/2 cup old-fashioned oats

1/2 cup tomato puree

2 tablespoons chopped fresh parsley

1/2 teaspoon Italian seasoning

1/2 teaspoon salt

1/4 teaspoon pepper

1 small onion, chopped (1/4 cup)

1 clove garlic, finely chopped

prep time:
15 minutes

start to finish:
**1 hour
45 minutes**

1 Heat oven to 350°F. In large bowl, mix all ingredients thoroughly. Press mixture evenly in ungreased 8×4- or 9×5-inch loaf pan.

2 Bake uncovered 1 hour 15 minutes to 1 hour 30 minutes or until no longer pink in center and meat thermometer inserted in center reads at least 160°F.

carb-bit

Lean ground turkey breast and old-fashioned oats help cut fat and keep moistness in this tasty version of the all-family favorite. Did you know? Old-fashioned oats are a whole grain.

1 serving: Cal. 160 (Cal. from Fat 70); Fat 8g (Sat. fat 2.5g); Chol. 55mg; Sodium 260mg; Net Carbohydrate 5g; Carbs. 6g (Fiber 1g); Pro. 18g | **% daily value:** Vit. A 6%; Vit. C 2%; Calc. 0%; Iron 10% | **exchanges:** 1/2 Starch, 2 1/2 Lean Meat | **CARB. CHOICES:** 1/2

Beef Stew, Bologna Style

1 1/2 lb beef boneless sirloin steak, about 1 inch thick

1 tablespoon olive or vegetable oil

4 oz sliced pancetta or lean bacon, cut into 1/2-inch pieces

1 medium onion, chopped (1/2 cup)

1 medium green bell pepper, chopped (1 cup)

2 cloves garlic, finely chopped

1 tablespoon chopped fresh parsley

1 cup sweet red wine or beef broth

1 tablespoon balsamic vinegar

1/4 teaspoon salt

1/4 teaspoon pepper

2 medium potatoes, cut into 1-inch pieces

1 medium carrot, thinly sliced (1/2 cup)

2 fresh or dried bay leaves

1 Remove fat from beef. Cut beef into 1-inch cubes.

2 In nonstick 4-quart Dutch oven, heat oil over medium heat. Cook pancetta, onion, bell pepper, garlic and parsley in oil about 10 minutes, stirring occasionally, until pancetta is brown.

3 Stir in beef and remaining ingredients. Heat to boiling; reduce heat. Cover and simmer about 1 hour, stirring occasionally, until beef is tender. Remove bay leaves.

Total Carbs **13g**

Net Carbs **11g**

prep time:
25 minutes

start to finish:
**1 hour
25 minutes**

1 serving: Cal. 230 (Cal. from Fat 80); Fat 9g (Sat. fat 2.5g); Chol. 65mg; Sodium 230mg; Net Carbohydrate 11g; Carbs. 13g (Fiber 2g); Pro. 26g | **% daily value:** Vit. A 40%; Vit. C 25%; Calc. 2%; Iron 20% | **exchanges:** 1/2 Other Carb., 3 1/2 Lean Meat | **CARB. CHOICES:** 1

Beef Stew, Bologna Style

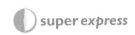
super express

Total Carbs **5g**
Net Carbs **3g**

prep time:
20 minutes

start to finish:
20 minutes

4 servings

Veal with Asparagus

I teaspoon vegetable oil

I tablespoon finely chopped shallot

I clove garlic, finely chopped

3/4 lb thin slices lean veal round steak or veal for scallopini

I cup sliced fresh mushrooms (3 oz)

1/3 cup dry white wine

2 teaspoons chopped fresh or 1/2 teaspoon dried thyme leaves

12 oz asparagus spears, cut into 1-inch pieces*

1 In 10-inch nonstick skillet, heat oil over medium-high heat. Cook shallot and garlic in oil, stirring frequently, until garlic is golden; reduce heat to medium. Add veal. Cook about 3 minutes, turning once, until light brown.

2 Stir in remaining ingredients. Heat to boiling; reduce heat. Cover and simmer about 12 minutes, stirring occasionally, until asparagus is crisp-tender.

*1 box (9 oz) frozen asparagus cuts, thawed, can be substituted for the fresh asparagus.

I serving: Cal. 120 (Cal. from Fat 40); Fat 4.5g (Sat. fat 1.5g); Chol. 55mg; Sodium 50mg; Net Carbohydrate 3g; Carbs. 5g (Fiber 2g); Pro. 16g | **% daily value:** Vit. A 15%; Vit. C 20%; Calc. 4%; Iron 8% | **exchanges:** I Vegetable, 2 Lean Meat | **CARB. CHOICES:** 0

Veal with Asparagus

Total Carbs **9g**
Net Carbs **9g**

prep time:
20 minutes

start to finish:
20 minutes

4 servings

Breaded Pork Chops

1/4 cup Reduced Fat Bisquick mix

7 saltine cracker squares, crushed (1/2 cup)

1/2 teaspoon seasoned salt

1/8 teaspoon pepper

1/4 cup fat-free cholesterol-free egg product

1 tablespoon water

4 pork boneless loin chops, 1/2 inch thick (about 1 lb)

1 In shallow dish, mix Bisquick mix, cracker crumbs, seasoned salt and pepper. In another shallow dish, mix egg product and water. Dip pork into egg mixture, then coat with Bisquick mixture.

2 Spray 12-inch skillet with cooking spray; heat over medium-high heat. Cook pork in skillet 8 to 10 minutes, turning once, until no longer pink in center.

1 serving: Cal. 240 (Cal. from Fat 90); Fat 10g (Sat. fat 3.5g); Chol. 70mg; Sodium 380mg; Net Carbohydrate 9g; Carbs. 9g (Fiber 0g); Pro. 28g | **% daily value:** Vit. A 0%; Vit. C 0%; Calc. 2%; Iron 10% | **exchanges:** 1/2 Starch, 3 1/2 Lean Meat | **CARB. CHOICES:** 1/2

Breaded Pork Chops

Southwestern Pork Chops

Total Carbs 0g
Net Carbs 0g

prep time:
10 minutes

start to finish:
**1 hour
20 minutes**

8 pork loin or rib chops, about 1/2 inch thick (about 2 lb)

1 tablespoon chili powder

1 teaspoon ground cumin

1/4 teaspoon ground red pepper (cayenne)

1/4 teaspoon salt

1 large clove garlic, finely chopped

1 Remove fat from pork. In small bowl, mix remaining ingredients; rub evenly on both sides of pork. Cover and refrigerate 1 hour to blend flavors.

2 Heat coals or gas grill for direct heat. Cover and grill pork over medium heat 8 to 10 minutes, turning frequently, until no longer pink when cut near bone.

1 serving: Cal. 130 (Cal. from Fat 60); Fat 6g (Sat. fat 2g); Chol. 50mg; Sodium 115mg; Net Carbohydrate 0g; Carbs. 0g (Fiber 0g); Pro. 18g | **% daily value:** Vit. A 8%; Vit. C 0%; Calc. 0%; Iron 6% | **exchanges:** 2 1/2 Lean Meat | **CARB. CHOICES:** 0

Southwestern Pork Chops

Total Carbs **19g**
Net Carbs **19g**

prep time:
30 minutes

start to finish:
30 minutes

4 servings

Honey-Mustard Pork Chops

1/4 cup honey

2 tablespoons Dijon mustard

1 tablespoon orange juice

**1 teaspoon chopped fresh or
1/4 teaspoon dried tarragon leaves**

1 teaspoon balsamic or cider vinegar

1/2 teaspoon white Worcestershire sauce

Dash of onion powder

4 pork butterfly loin chops, 1 inch thick (about 1 lb)

1 Brush grill rack with vegetable oil. Heat coals or gas grill for direct heat. In small bowl, mix all ingredients except pork.

2 Cover and grill pork over medium heat 14 to 16 minutes, brushing occasionally with honey-mustard glaze and turning once, until no longer pink in center. Discard any remaining glaze.

1 serving: Cal. 270 (Cal. from Fat 90); Fat 10g (Sat. fat 3g); Chol. 75mg; Sodium 240mg; Net Carbohydrate 19g; Carbs. 19g (Fiber 0g); Pro. 27g | **% daily value:** Vit. A 0%; Vit. C 0%; Calc. 0%; Iron 6% | **exchanges:** 1 Other Carb., 4 Lean Meat | **CARB. CHOICES:** 1

4 servings

Greek Honey and Lemon Pork Chops

4 pork loin chops or ribs, 1/2 inch thick (about 1 lb)

1 tablespoon all-purpose Greek seasoning

1 teaspoon grated lemon peel

2 tablespoons lemon juice

3 tablespoons honey

1 Set oven control to broil. Place pork on rack in broiler pan. In small bowl, mix remaining ingredients. Brush honey mixture evenly on tops of pork chops.

2 Broil pork with tops 4 to 6 inches from heat 7 to 8 minutes, turning once and brushing with honey mixture, until no longer pink when cut near bone. Discard any remaining honey mixture.

Total Carbs **14g**
Net Carbs **14g**

prep time:
15 minutes

start to finish:
15 minutes

carb-bit

Make a salad using fresh spinach, tomatoes and Kalamata olives for a bit of Mediterranean inspiration.

1 serving: Cal. 230 (Cal. from Fat 80); Fat 9g (Sat. fat 3g); Chol. 70mg; Sodium 45mg; Net Carbohydrate 14g; Carbs. 14g (Fiber 0g); Pro. 24g | **% daily value:** Vit. A 0%; Vit. C 2%; Calc. 2%; Iron 8% | **exchanges:** 1 Other Carb., 3 1/2 Lean Meat | **CARB. CHOICES:** 1

Total Carbs **19g**
Net Carbs **19g**

prep time:
20 minutes

start to finish:
20 minutes

carb-bit

Look for sugar-free spreadable fruit, jam or preserves if you'd like to slash the carbs.

4 servings

Pork Medallions with Hot Pineapple Glaze

1 lb pork tenderloin

1/4 teaspoon salt

1/3 cup pineapple or orange marmalade spreadable fruit

2 teaspoons Worcestershire sauce

2 teaspoons cider vinegar

1/2 teaspoon grated gingerroot

1/4 teaspoon crushed red pepper flakes, if desired

1 Cut pork into 1/4-inch slices. Sprinkle both sides of pork with salt.

2 Heat 12-inch nonstick skillet over medium-high heat. Cook pork in skillet 5 to 6 minutes, turning once, until no longer pink in center. Remove pork from skillet; keep warm.

3 In skillet, mix remaining ingredients; heat to boiling. Boil and stir 1 minute. Serve sauce over pork.

1 serving: Cal. 220 (Cal. from Fat 40); Fat 4.5g (Sat. fat 1.5g); Chol. 70mg; Sodium 230mg; Net Carbohydrate 19g; Carbs. 19g (Fiber 0g); Pro. 26g | **% daily value:** Vit. A 0%; Vit. C 2%; Calc. 0%; Iron 10% | **exchanges:** 1 Other Carb., 3 1/2 Very Lean Meat, 1/2 Fat | **CARB. CHOICES:** 1

super express

Garlicky Pork with Basil

Total Carbs 1g
Net Carbs 1g

prep time:
25 minutes

start to finish:
25 minutes

3/4 lb pork tenderloin

1 teaspoon vegetable oil

1/4 cup chopped fresh or 1 tablespoon plus 1 teaspoon dried basil leaves

1/4 cup fat-free chicken broth

1/8 teaspoon ground red pepper (cayenne)

4 cloves garlic, finely chopped

1 Cut pork crosswise into 8 pieces. Between pieces of plastic wrap or waxed paper, place pork pieces; gently pound with flat side of meat mallet or rolling pin until about 1/4 inch thick.

2 In 10-inch nonstick skillet, heat oil over medium-high heat. Cook pork in oil about 3 minutes, turning once, until brown. Stir in remaining ingredients. Heat to boiling; reduce heat. Cover and simmer about 5 minutes or until pork is no longer pink in center.

1 serving: Cal. 120 (Cal. from Fat 40); Fat 4.5g (Sat. fat 1.5g); Chol. 55mg; Sodium 70mg; Net Carbohydrate 1g; Carbs. 1g (Fiber 0g); Pro. 19g | **% daily value:** Vit. A 4%; Vit. C 0%; Calc. 0%; Iron 6% | **exchanges:** 2 1/2 Lean Meat | **CARB. CHOICES:** 0

Total Carbs **12g**
Net Carbs **10g**

prep time:
50 minutes

start to finish:
50 minutes

Pork with Rich Vegetable Gravy

1 lb pork tenderloin	1 cup sliced fresh mushrooms (3 oz)
1/2 teaspoon seasoned salt	1 can (14 oz) beef broth
1 tablespoon butter or margarine	2 tablespoons all-purpose flour
2 medium carrots, sliced (1 cup)	1 tablespoon ketchup
1 medium onion, chopped (1/2 cup)	2 tablespoons dry sherry, if desired
1 medium stalk celery, sliced (1/2 cup)	1/4 teaspoon dried thyme leaves

1 Spray 12-inch skillet with cooking spray; heat over medium-high heat. Cut pork into 1/4-inch slices. Sprinkle pork with seasoned salt. Cook pork in skillet 4 to 6 minutes, turning once, until brown. Remove pork from skillet.

2 To skillet, add butter, carrots, onion and celery. Cook 4 to 5 minutes, stirring occasionally, until vegetables are crisp-tender. Stir in mushrooms. Cook 2 minutes.

3 In small bowl, mix broth and flour until smooth. Stir broth mixture, ketchup, sherry and thyme into vegetable mixture. Cook uncovered about 10 minutes, stirring occasionally, until vegetables are tender.

4 Stir in pork. Cook 4 to 5 minutes or until pork is no longer pink in center.

1 serving: Cal. 220 (Cal. from Fat 70); Fat 8g (Sat. fat 3g); Chol. 80mg; Sodium 740mg; Net Carbohydrate 10g; Carbs. 12g (Fiber 2g); Pro. 28g | **% daily value:** Vit. A 120%; Vit. C 6%; Calc. 4%; Iron 10% | **exchanges:** 1/2 Other Carb., 4 Lean Meat | **CARB. CHOICES:** 1/2

4 servings

Caramelized Pork Slices

1 lb pork tenderloin

2 cloves garlic, finely chopped

2 tablespoons packed brown sugar

1 tablespoon orange juice

1 tablespoon molasses

1/2 teaspoon salt

1/4 teaspoon pepper

prep time:
20 minutes

start to finish:
20 minutes

1 Cut pork into 1/2-inch slices. Heat 10-inch nonstick skillet over medium-high heat. Cook pork and garlic in skillet 6 to 8 minutes, turning occasionally, until pork is no longer pink in center. Drain if necessary.

2 Stir in remaining ingredients. Cook until mixture thickens and coats pork.

1 serving: Cal. 190 (Cal. from Fat 40); Fat 4.5g (Sat. fat 1.5g); Chol. 70mg; Sodium 350mg; Net Carbohydrate 12g; Carbs. 12g (Fiber 0g); Pro. 26g | **% daily value:** Vit. A 0%; Vit. C 0%; Calc. 2%; Iron 10% | **exchanges:** 1 Other Carb., 3 1/2 Very Lean Meat, 1/2 Fat | **CARB. CHOICES:** 1

Caribbean Pork Tenderloin

2 cups cut-up assorted fresh fruit (cantaloupe, honeydew melon, grapes, papaya, mango)

I tablespoon chopped fresh cilantro

I to 2 teaspoons lime juice

I tablespoon ground cinnamon

4 teaspoons ground nutmeg

4 teaspoons ground cumin

4 teaspoons garlic salt

1/4 to 1/2 teaspoon ground red pepper (cayenne)

I 1/4 lb pork tenderloin

1 In small glass or plastic bowl, mix fruit, cilantro and lime juice. Cover and refrigerate until serving.

2 In small bowl, mix remaining ingredients except pork. In heavy-duty resealable plastic food-storage bag, place pork. Sprinkle pork with spice mixture; turn bag several times to coat pork. Seal bag; refrigerate 15 minutes.

3 Heat coals or gas grill for direct heat. Remove pork from bag. Cover and grill pork over medium heat 15 to 20 minutes, turning frequently, until pork has slight blush of pink in center and thermometer inserted in center of thickest part of pork reads 160°F. Serve with fruit mixture.

Total Carbs **15g**
Net Carbs **13g**

prep time: **45 minutes**

start to finish: **1 hour**

carb-bit

Melon weighs in with only 6 to 8 grams of carb per half cup. Another benefit? You can make this recipe even easier, by using precut mixed fruit from the produce section or the deli section of your supermarket.

I serving: Cal. 260 (Cal. from Fat 60); Fat 7g (Sat. fat 2.5g); Chol. 90mg; Sodium 1040mg; Net Carbohydrate 13g; Carbs. 15g (Fiber 2g); Pro. 33g | **% daily value:** Vit. A 25%; Vit. C 20%; Calc. 6%; Iron 20% | **exchanges:** I Fruit, 4 1/2 Very Lean Meat, I Fat | **CARB. CHOICES:** I

Caribbean Pork Tenderloin

Italian Roasted Pork Tenderloin

Total Carbs **0g**
Net Carbs **0g**

prep time:
10 minutes

start to finish:
45 minutes

I teaspoon olive or vegetable oil	1/4 teaspoon pepper
1/2 teaspoon salt	I clove garlic, finely chopped
1/2 teaspoon fennel seed, crushed	2 pork tenderloins (about 3/4 lb each)

1 Heat oven to 375°F. Spray rack of roasting pan with cooking spray. In small bowl, mash all ingredients except pork into a paste. Rub paste on pork.

2 Place pork on rack in shallow roasting pan. Insert meat thermometer so tip is in center of thickest part of pork. Bake uncovered about 35 minutes or until pork has slight blush of pink in center and thermometer reads 160°F.

I serving: Cal. 150 (Cal. from Fat 45); Fat 5g (Sat. fat 1.5g); Chol. 70mg; Sodium 250mg; Net Carbohydrate 0g; Carbs. 0g (Fiber 0g); Pro. 26g | **% daily value:** Vit. A 0%; Vit. C 0%; Calc. 0%; Iron 8% | **exchanges:** 3 1/2 Very Lean Meat, 1/2 Fat | **CARB. CHOICES:** 0

6 servings

Mustard Lamb Chops

6 lamb sirloin or shoulder chops, about 3/4 inch thick (about 2 lb)

1 tablespoon chopped fresh or 1 teaspoon dried thyme leaves

2 tablespoons Dijon mustard

1/4 teaspoon salt

Total Carbs **0g**
Net Carbs **0g**

prep time:
25 minutes

start to finish:
25 minutes

1 Set oven control to broil. Remove fat from lamb. Place lamb on rack in broiler pan. In small bowl, mix remaining ingredients. Brush half of the mustard mixture evenly over lamb chops.

2 Broil lamb with tops 3 to 4 inches from heat about 4 minutes or until brown. Turn lamb; brush with remaining mustard mixture. Broil 5 to 7 minutes longer for medium doneness (160°F).

1 serving: Cal. 120 (Cal. from Fat 50); Fat 6g (Sat. fat 2g); Chol. 55mg; Sodium 270mg; Net Carbohydrate 0g; Carbs. 0g (Fiber 0g); Pro. 17g | **% daily value:** Vit. A 0%; Vit. C 0%; Calc. 0%; Iron 8% | **exchanges:** 2 1/2 Lean Meat | **CARB. CHOICES:** 0

Total Carbs **10g**
Net Carbs **10g**

prep time:
20 minutes

start to finish:
20 minutes

4 servings

Lamb with Creamy Mint Sauce

2/3 cup plain fat-free yogurt

1/4 cup firmly packed fresh mint leaves

2 tablespoons sugar

4 lamb loin chops, about 1 inch thick (1 lb)

1 In blender or food processor, place yogurt, mint and sugar. Cover and blend on medium speed, stopping blender occasionally to scrape sides, until mint leaves are finely chopped.

2 Set oven control to broil. Spray broiler pan rack with cooking spray. Remove fat from lamb. Place lamb on rack in broiler pan. Broil with tops 2 to 3 inches from heat 12 to 14 minutes, turning after 6 minutes, for medium doneness (160°F). Serve with sauce.

1 serving: Cal. 170 (Cal. from Fat 50); Fat 6g (Sat. fat 2g); Chol. 60mg; Sodium 75mg; Net Carbohydrate 10g; Carbs. 10g (Fiber 0g); Pro. 20g | **% daily value:** Vit. A 0%; Vit. C 0%; Calc. 10%; Iron 8% | **exchanges:** 1/2 Other Carb., 1/2 Skim Milk, 2 Lean Meat | **CARB. CHOICES:** 1/2

4 Chicken and Turkey

Italian Chicken Packets   108

Sesame Ginger Chicken   110

Lemon Thyme Chicken Breasts   112

Grilled Citrus Chicken   114

Caribbean Chicken Kabobs   116

Teriyaki Chicken Kabobs   118

Hot Seared Chicken   119

Italian Chicken Salad   120

Basil and Prosciutto Chicken   122

Easy Salsa Chicken   124

Wild Mushroom Herbed
    Chicken   125

Moroccan Chicken   126

Chicken in Olive-Wine Sauce   127

Chicken Marsala   128

Summer Garden Chicken Stir-Fry   130

Balsamic Chicken   131

Chicken and Strawberry-Spinach
    Salad   132

Chicken with Savory Sauce   134

Crunchy Herbed Baked
    Chicken Breasts   136

Baked Oregano Chicken   137

Crunchy Garlic Chicken   138

Oven-Fried Chicken Nuggets   139

Thai Chicken with Cucumber–Red
    Onion Relish   140

Fiesta Chicken and Rice   141

Southwestern Chicken BLT Salad   142

Turkey Tenderloins and Mixed Sweet
    Peppers   143

California-Style Turkey Patties with Corn
    and Tomato Relish   144

Honey-Mustard Turkey with
    Snap Peas   146

◑ = **super express** ready in 30 minutes or less

Italian Chicken Packets

Total Carbs 8g
Net Carbs 7g

prep time:
35 minutes

start to finish:
35 minutes

4 boneless skinless chicken breast halves (about 1 1/4 lb)

1 medium yellow bell pepper, cut into 4 wedges

4 roma (plum) tomatoes, cut in half

1 small red onion, cut into 8 wedges

1/2 cup reduced-fat Italian dressing

1 Heat coals or gas grill for direct heat. Cut four 18×12-inch pieces of heavy-duty foil. Place 1 chicken breast half, 1 bell pepper wedge, 2 tomato halves and 2 onion wedges on one side of each foil piece. Pour 2 tablespoons dressing over chicken and vegetable mixture on each packet.

2 Fold foil over chicken and vegetables so edges meet. Seal edges, making tight 1/2-inch fold, fold again. Allow space on sides for circulation and expansion.

3 Cover and grill packets over medium heat 18 to 22 minutes, rotating packets 1/2 turn after 10 minutes, until juice of chicken is no longer pink when centers of thickest pieces are cut. Place packets on plates. Cut large X across tops of packets; fold back foil.

1 serving: Cal. 250 (Cal. from Fat 90); Fat 10g (Sat. fat 2g); Chol. 85mg; Sodium 470mg; Net Carbohydrate 7g; Carbs. 8g (Fiber 1g); Pro. 32g | **% daily value:** Vit. A 10%; Vit. C 60%; Calc. 2%; Iron 8% | **exchanges:** 1 Vegetable, 4 1/2 Very Lean Meat, 1 1/2 Fat | **CARB. CHOICES:** 1/2

Italian Chicken Packets

Total Carbs **2g**
Net Carbs **2g**

prep time:
25 minutes

start to finish:
25 minutes

4 servings

Sesame Ginger Chicken

2 tablespoons teriyaki sauce

1 tablespoon sesame seed, toasted*

1 teaspoon ground ginger

4 boneless skinless chicken breast halves (about 1 1/4 lb)

1 Brush grill rack with vegetable oil. Heat coals or gas grill for direct heat. In small bowl, mix teriyaki sauce, sesame seed and ginger.

2 Cover and grill chicken over medium heat 15 to 20 minutes, brushing frequently with sauce mixture and turning after 10 minutes, until juice is no longer pink when centers of thickest pieces are cut. Discard any remaining sauce mixture.

*To toast sesame seed, cook in ungreased heavy skillet over medium-low heat 5 to 7 minutes, stirring frequently until browning begins, then stirring constantly until golden brown.

1 serving: Cal. 190 (Cal. from Fat 50); Fat 6g (Sat. fat 1.5g); Chol. 85mg; Sodium 420mg; Net Carbohydrate 2g; Carbs. 2g (Fiber 0g); Pro. 32g | **% daily value:** Vit. A 0%; Vit. C 0%; Calc. 2%; Iron 8% | **exchanges:** 4 Very Lean Meat, 1 Fat | **CARB. CHOICES:** 0

Sesame Ginger Chicken

Lemon Thyme Chicken Breasts

1 tablespoon freshly grated lemon peel

4 teaspoons chopped fresh or 1 1/2 teaspoons dried thyme leaves

2 teaspoons garlic salt

1/2 teaspoon pepper

4 boneless skinless chicken breast halves (about 1 1/4 lb)

1. If using charcoal grill, place drip pan directly under grilling area, and arrange coals around edge of firebox. Spray grill rack with cooking spray. Heat coals or gas grill for indirect heat.

2. In small bowl, mix all ingredients except chicken. Sprinkle mixture over chicken.

3. Cover and grill chicken over drip pan or over unheated side of gas grill over medium-high heat 15 to 20 minutes, turning once, until chicken is no longer pink when centers of thickest pieces are cut. Garnish with additional fresh thyme if desired.

1 serving: Cal. 170 (Cal. from Fat 40); Fat 4.5g (Sat. fat 1.5g); Chol. 85mg; Sodium 560mg; Net Carbohydrate 1g; Carbs. 1g (Fiber 0g); Pro. 31g | **% daily value:** Vit. A 0%; Vit. C 4%; Calc. 2%; Iron 8% | **exchanges:** 4 1/2 Very Lean Meat, 1/2 Fat | **CARB. CHOICES:** 0

Lemon Thyme Chicken Breasts

Grilled Citrus Chicken

Total Carbs **10g**
Net Carbs **10g**

prep time:
35 minutes

start to finish:
**2 hours
35 minutes**

1/2 cup frozen (thawed) orange juice concentrate

2 tablespoons olive or vegetable oil

1/4 cup lemon juice

2 tablespoons grated orange peel

1/2 teaspoon salt

1 clove garlic, finely chopped

6 boneless skinless chicken breast halves (about 1 3/4 lb)

1 In shallow glass or plastic dish or resealable plastic food-storage bag, mix all ingredients except chicken. Add chicken; turn to coat. Cover dish or seal bag and refrigerate, turning chicken occasionally, at least 2 hours but no longer than 24 hours.

2 Heat coals or gas grill for direct heat. Remove chicken from marinade; reserve marinade. Cover and grill chicken over medium heat 15 to 20 minutes, turning and brushing with marinade occasionally, until juice of chicken is no longer pink when centers of thickest pieces are cut.

3 Heat remaining marinade to boiling in 1-quart saucepan; boil and stir 1 minute. Serve with chicken.

1 serving: Cal. 240 (Cal. from Fat 80); Fat 9g (Sat. fat 2g); Chol. 80mg; Sodium 270mg; Net Carbohydrate 10g; Carbs. 10g (Fiber 0g); Pro. 30g | **% daily value:** Vit. A 2%; Vit. C 30%; Calc. 2%; Iron 6% | **exchanges:** 1/2 Other Carb., 4 Very Lean Meat, 1 1/2 Fat | **CARB. CHOICES:** 1/2

Grilled Citrus Chicken

Caribbean Chicken Kabobs

prep time:
35 minutes

start to finish:
35 minutes

I 3/4 lb boneless skinless chicken breast halves

1/4 cup vegetable oil

3 tablespoons Caribbean jerk seasoning (dry)

I small pineapple, rind removed, pineapple cut into I-inch cubes

I medium red bell pepper, cut into I-inch pieces

I small red onion, cut into I-inch pieces

1 Brush grill rack with vegetable oil. Heat coals or gas grill for direct heat. Remove fat from chicken. Cut chicken into 1 1/2-inch pieces.

2 Brush chicken with 2 tablespoons of the oil. In resealable plastic food-storage bag, place chicken and jerk seasoning; seal bag. Shake bag to coat chicken with seasoning. On each of eight 12-inch metal skewers, thread chicken, pineapple, bell pepper and onion alternately, leaving 1/4-inch space between each piece. Brush kabobs with remaining 2 tablespoons oil.

3 Cover and grill kabobs over medium heat 15 to 20 minutes, turning once, until chicken is no longer pink in center.

I serving: Cal. 210 (Cal. from Fat 90); Fat 10g (Sat. fat 2g); Chol. 60mg; Sodium 370mg; Net Carbohydrate 8g; Carbs. 9g (Fiber Ig); Pro. 22g | **% daily value:** Vit. A 20%; Vit. C 30%; Calc. 0%; Iron 6% | **exchanges:** I/2 Fruit, 3 Very Lean Meat, I I/2 Fat | **CARB. CHOICES:** I/2

Caribbean Chicken Kabobs

Total Carbs **15g**
Net Carbs **13g**

prep time:
30 minutes

start to finish:
50 minutes

4 servings

Teriyaki Chicken Kabobs

I lb boneless skinless chicken breast halves

2 tablespoons teriyaki sauce

1/2 teaspoon sugar

I 1/2 teaspoons olive or vegetable oil

1/4 teaspoon ground ginger

I small clove garlic, finely chopped

I can (8 oz) pineapple chunks, drained

I medium green bell pepper, cut into I 1/2-inch pieces

2 small onions, cut into fourths

1 Remove fat from chicken. Cut chicken into 1-inch pieces. In glass or plastic dish or resealable plastic food-storage bag, mix chicken, teriyaki sauce, sugar, oil, ginger and garlic. Cover dish or seal bag and refrigerate 20 minutes.

2 Heat coals or gas grill for direct heat. Remove chicken from marinade; reserve marinade. On each of four 15-inch metal skewers, thread 4 or 5 chicken pieces, pineapple, bell pepper and onion alternately, leaving 1/4-inch space between each piece.

3 Cover and grill kabobs over medium heat 10 to 15 minutes, turning and brushing 2 or 3 times with marinade, until chicken is no longer pink in center. Discard any remaining marinade. Serve kabobs with additional teriyaki sauce if desired.

I serving: Cal. 210 (Cal. from Fat 50); Fat 6g (Sat. fat 1.5g); Chol. 70mg; Sodium 410mg; Net Carbohydrate 13g; Carbs. 15g (Fiber 2g); Pro. 26g | **% daily value:** Vit. A 4%; Vit. C 30%; Calc. 4%; Iron 8% | **exchanges:** I Other Carb., 3 1/2 Very Lean Meat, I Fat | **CARB. CHOICES:** I

I 18   BETTY CROCKER low-carb lifestyle cookbook

4 servings

Hot Seared Chicken

4 boneless skinless chicken breast halves (about 1 1/4 lb)

1 tablespoon lime juice

1 1/2 teaspoons blackened seasoning mixture or jerk seasoning (dry)

1/8 teaspoon ground cumin

2 teaspoons butter or margarine

1/4 cup water

Hot cooked brown rice, if desired

1 Remove fat from chicken. In small bowl, mix 1 1/2 teaspoons of the lime juice, the seasoning mixture and cumin. Rub mixture evenly over both sides of chicken.

2 Heat 10-inch nonstick skillet over medium-high heat. Melt butter in skillet. Cook chicken in butter about 8 minutes, turning once, until chicken is no longer pink when centers of thickest pieces are cut. Remove chicken from skillet; keep warm.

3 Add remaining 1 1/2 teaspoons lime juice and the water to chicken drippings in skillet. Heat to boiling. Boil and stir about 45 seconds or until liquid is reduced to about 2 tablespoons. Spoon sauce over chicken. Serve with rice.

Total Carbs 0g
Net Carbs 0g

prep time:
20 minutes

start to finish:
20 minutes

1 serving: Cal. 180 (Cal. from Fat 60); Fat 6g (Sat. fat 2.5g); Chol. 90mg; Sodium 200mg; Net Carbohydrate 0g; Carbs. 0g (Fiber 0g); Pro. 31g | **% daily value:** Vit. A 2%; Vit. C 0%; Calc. 0%; Iron 6% | **exchanges:** 4 1/2 Very Lean Meat, 1/2 Fat | **CARB. CHOICES:** 0

Italian Chicken Salad

Total Carbs **8g**
Net Carbs **6g**

prep time:
30 minutes

start to finish:
45 minutes

1/3 cup raspberry vinegar

2 tablespoons balsamic vinegar

1/4 cup water

1 package (0.7 oz) Italian dressing mix

1 tablespoon olive or vegetable oil

4 boneless skinless chicken breast halves (about 1 1/4 lb)

6 cups bite-size pieces mixed salad greens

2 roma (plum) tomatoes, chopped (2/3 cup)

1 In medium bowl, mix vinegars and water. Stir in dressing mix. Stir in oil. Divide dressing mixture in half.

2 In shallow glass or plastic dish or heavy-duty resealable plastic food-storage bag, place chicken. Pour half of the dressing mixture over chicken; turn chicken to coat. Cover dish or seal bag and refrigerate 15 minutes. Cover and refrigerate remaining dressing mixture.

3 Heat coals or gas grill for direct heat. Remove chicken from marinade; reserve marinade. Cover and grill chicken over medium heat 15 to 20 minutes, turning and brushing with marinade occasionally, until juice of chicken is no longer pink when centers of thickest piece are cut. Discard any remaining marinade.

4 Cut chicken into slices. Serve chicken on salad greens with remaining dressing mixture. Top with tomatoes.

1 serving: Cal. 230 (Cal. from Fat 70); Fat 8g (Sat. fat 2g); Chol. 85mg; Sodium 740mg; Net Carbohydrate 6g; Carbs. 8g (Fiber 2g); Pro. 33g | **% daily value:** Vit. A 60%; Vit. C 35%; Calc. 6%; Iron 15% | **exchanges:** 1 1/2 Vegetable, 4 1/2 Very Lean Meat, 1 Fat | **CARB. CHOICES:** 1/2

Italian Chicken Salad

super *express*

Total Carbs **0g**
Net Carbs **0g**

prep time:
30 minutes

start to finish:
30 minutes

4 servings

Basil and Prosciutto Chicken

I tablespoon vegetable oil

4 boneless skinless chicken breast halves (about I 1/4 lb)

4 teaspoons Dijon mustard

4 thin slices prosciutto or fully cooked ham (4 oz)

1/4 cup shredded part-skim mozzarella cheese (I oz)

4 fresh basil leaves

1 In 10-inch skillet, heat oil over medium heat. Cook chicken in oil 6 minutes. Turn chicken; brush with mustard and top with prosciutto. Cook 6 to 8 minutes longer or until juice of chicken is no longer pink when centers of thickest pieces are cut.

2 Place cheese and basil on chicken. Cook about 2 minutes or until cheese is melted.

I serving: Cal. 270 (Cal. from Fat 110); Fat 12g (Sat. fat 3.5g); Chol. 105mg; Sodium 660mg; Net Carbohydrate 0g; Carbs. 0g (Fiber 0g); Pro. 40g | **% daily value:** Vit. A 2%; Vit. C 0%; Calc. 8%; Iron 8% | **exchanges:** 6 Very Lean Meat, 1 1/2 Fat | **CARB. CHOICES:** 0

Basil and Prosciutto Chicken

Total Carbs **15g**
Net Carbs **12g**

prep time:
20 minutes

start to finish:
20 minutes

4 servings

Easy Salsa Chicken

1 lb boneless skinless chicken breast halves

2 tablespoons butter or margarine

1 medium zucchini, sliced (2 cups)

1 cup sliced fresh mushrooms (3 oz)

2 1/2 cups salsa or picante sauce

2 teaspoons sugar

1 Remove fat from chicken. Cut chicken into 1-inch pieces. In 10-inch skillet, melt butter over medium heat. Cook chicken in butter 4 minutes, stirring occasionally.

2 Stir in zucchini and mushrooms. Cook, stirring occasionally, until chicken is no longer pink in center and vegetables are tender.

3 Stir in salsa and sugar. Cook about 5 minutes, stirring occasionally, until hot.

1 serving: Cal. 250 (Cal. from Fat 90); Fat 10g (Sat. fat 4g); Chol. 85mg; Sodium 810mg; Net Carbohydrate 12g; Carbs. 15g (Fiber 3g); Pro. 28g | **% daily value:** Vit. A 35%; Vit. C 25%; Calc. 8%; Iron 15% | **exchanges:** 1/2 Other Carb., 1 Vegetable, 4 Very Lean Meat, 1 1/2 Fat | **CARB. CHOICES:** 1

6 servings

Wild Mushroom Herbed Chicken

1 tablespoon olive or vegetable oil

6 boneless skinless chicken breast halves (about 1 3/4 lb)

3/4 lb assorted wild mushrooms (oyster, shiitake, chanterelle), coarsely chopped (5 cups)

1 medium leek, sliced (2 cups)

3 cloves garlic, finely chopped

1 can (14 oz) chicken broth

1/2 cup dry white wine or chicken broth

2 tablespoons cornstarch

1/2 teaspoon dried thyme leaves

1 Remove fat from chicken. In 12-inch nonstick skillet, heat oil over medium heat. Cook chicken in oil about 12 minutes, turning once, until juice is no longer pink when centers of thickest pieces are cut. Remove chicken from skillet; keep warm.

2 In same skillet, cook mushrooms, leek and garlic about 3 minutes, stirring frequently, until leek is tender. In medium bowl, mix remaining ingredients; stir into mushroom mixture. Heat to boiling, stirring occasionally. Boil and stir about 1 minute or until slightly thickened. Add chicken; heat through.

Total Carbs **10g**
Net Carbs **9g**

prep time:
30 minutes

start to finish:
30 minutes

carb-bit

Wild mushrooms have a fuller and more robust flavor than regular white or button mushrooms and 4 ounces have roughly 6 grams of carbs.

1 serving: Cal. 230 (Cal. from Fat 60); Fat 7g (Sat. fat 1.5g); Chol. 80mg; Sodium 360mg; Net Carbohydrate 9g; Carbs. 10g (Fiber 1g); Pro. 33g | **% daily value:** Vit. A 10%; Vit. C 4%; Calc. 4%; Iron 15% | **exchanges:** 1 Vegetable, 4 1/2 Very Lean Meat, 1 Fat | **CARB. CHOICES:** 1/2

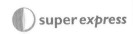
Total Carbs **11g**
Net Carbs **9g**

prep time:
20 minutes

start to finish:
30 minutes

4 servings

Moroccan Chicken

4 boneless skinless chicken breast halves (about 1 1/4 lb)

1 can (14.5 oz) Italian-style stewed tomatoes

1 medium onion, cut into 8 wedges and separated

3 cloves garlic, finely chopped

1/2 cup dry white wine or chicken broth

1/2 teaspoon ground cumin

1/2 teaspoon ground ginger

1/2 teaspoon crushed red pepper flakes

Hot cooked couscous, if desired

Chopped fresh parsley, if desired

Greek or Italian black olives, pitted, sliced, if desired

1 Remove fat from chicken. Drain tomatoes, reserving liquid. Cut up tomatoes.

2 In 12-inch nonstick skillet, heat chicken, tomatoes, tomato liquid, onion, garlic, wine, cumin, ginger and red pepper flakes to boiling; reduce heat. Cover and simmer about 10 minutes or until juice of chicken is no longer pink when centers of thickest pieces are cut. Remove chicken; keep warm.

3 Heat sauce to boiling; reduce heat. Simmer uncovered 2 minutes. Serve chicken over couscous. Pour sauce over chicken. Sprinkle with parsley and olives.

1 serving: Cal. 210 (Cal. from Fat 45); Fat 5g (Sat. fat 1.5g); Chol. 85mg; Sodium 360mg; Net Carbohydrate 9g; Carbs. 11g (Fiber 2g); Pro. 32g | **% daily value:** Vit. A 8%; Vit. C 10%; Calc. 6%; Iron 10% | **exchanges:** 1/2 Other Carb., 1 Vegetable, 4 Very Lean Meat, 1/2 Fat | **CARB. CHOICES:** 1

4 servings

Chicken in Olive-Wine Sauce

Total Carbs **8g**
Net Carbs **7g**

prep time:
25 minutes

start to finish:
35 minutes

2 slices bacon, cut into 1-inch pieces

1 medium onion, chopped (1/2 cup)

2 cloves garlic, finely chopped

**1 tablespoon chopped fresh or
1 teaspoon dried rosemary leaves,
crumbled**

**4 boneless skinless chicken breast
halves (about 1 1/4 lb)**

1/3 cup pimiento-stuffed olives

1/2 cup dry red wine or chicken broth

3/4 cup seasoned croutons

1 tablespoon chopped fresh parsley

1 In 10-inch skillet, cook bacon, onion, garlic and rosemary over medium-high heat about 8 minutes, stirring occasionally, until bacon is crisp. Remove bacon with slotted spoon; set aside.

2 Add chicken to skillet. Cook about 5 minutes, turning frequently, until chicken is brown. Add olives, wine and bacon. Cover and cook about 12 minutes or until juice of chicken is no longer pink when centers of thickest pieces are cut.

3 Place chicken mixture on serving platter. Sprinkle with croutons and parsley.

1 serving: Cal. 250 (Cal. from Fat 90); Fat 10g (Sat. fat 2.5g); Chol. 90mg; Sodium 430mg; Net Carbohydrate 7g; Carbs. 8g (Fiber 1g); Pro. 34g | **% daily value:** Vit. A 4%; Vit. C 2%; Calc. 4%; Iron 8% | **exchanges:** 1/2 Starch, 4 1/2 Very Lean Meat, 1 1/2 Fat | **CARB. CHOICES:** 1/2

super *express*

Total Carbs **8g**
Net Carbs **8g**

prep time:
25 minutes

start to finish:
25 minutes

4 servings

Chicken Marsala

4 boneless skinless chicken breast halves (about 1 1/4 lb)

1/4 cup all-purpose flour

1/4 teaspoon salt

1/4 teaspoon pepper

1 tablespoon olive or vegetable oil

2 cloves garlic, finely chopped

1/4 cup chopped fresh parsley or 1 tablespoon parsley flakes

1 cup sliced fresh mushrooms (3 oz)

1/2 cup dry Marsala wine or chicken broth

1 Between pieces of plastic wrap or waxed paper, place each chicken breast half smooth side down; gently pound with flat side of meat mallet or rolling pin until about 1/4 inch thick. In shallow dish, mix flour, salt and pepper. Coat chicken with flour mixture; shake off excess flour.

2 In 10-inch nonstick skillet, heat oil over medium-high heat. Cook garlic and parsley in oil 5 minutes, stirring frequently.

3 Add chicken to skillet. Cook, turning once, until brown. Add mushrooms and wine. Cook 8 to 10 minutes, turning chicken once, until chicken is no longer pink in center.

1 serving: Cal. 230 (Cal. from Fat 70); Fat 8g (Sat. fat 2g); Chol. 85mg; Sodium 230mg; Net Carbohydrate 8g; Carbs. 8g (Fiber 0g); Pro. 33g | **% daily value:** Vit. A 8%; Vit. C 4%; Calc. 2%; Iron 10% | **exchanges:** 1/2 Starch, 4 1/2 Very Lean Meat, 1 Fat | **CARB. CHOICES:** 1/2

Chicken Marsala

Total Carbs **15g**
Net Carbs **11g**

prep time:
30 minutes

start to finish:
30 minutes

4 servings

Summer Garden Chicken Stir-Fry

I lb boneless skinless chicken breast halves

2 cloves garlic, finely chopped

2 teaspoons finely chopped gingerroot

I medium onion, cut into thin wedges

I cup baby-cut carrots, cut lengthwise in half

I cup fat-free chicken broth

3 tablespoons reduced-sodium soy sauce

2 to 3 teaspoons sugar

2 cups broccoli flowerets

I cup sliced fresh mushrooms (3 oz)

1/2 cup chopped red bell pepper

2 teaspoons cornstarch

Hot cooked brown rice, if desired

1 Remove fat from chicken. Cut chicken into 1-inch pieces. Heat 12-inch nonstick skillet over medium-high heat. Add chicken, garlic and gingerroot; cook and stir 2 to 3 minutes or until chicken is brown.

2 Stir in onion, carrots, 3/4 cup of the broth, the soy sauce and sugar. Cover and cook over medium heat 5 minutes, stirring occasionally.

3 Stir in broccoli, mushrooms and bell pepper. Cover and cook about 5 minutes, stirring occasionally, until chicken is no longer pink in center and vegetables are crisp-tender.

4 In small bowl, mix cornstarch and remaining 1/4 cup broth; stir into chicken mixture. Cook, stirring frequently, until sauce is thickened. Serve over rice.

I serving: Cal. 200 (Cal. from Fat 35); Fat 4g (Sat. fat 1g); Chol. 70mg; Sodium 610mg; Net Carbohydrate 11g; Carbs. 15g (Fiber 4g); Pro. 28g | **% daily value:** Vit. A 150%; Vit. C 70%; Calc. 6%; Iron 10% | **exchanges:** 1/2 Starch, 1 Vegetable, 3 1/2 Very Lean Meat, 1/2 Fat | **CARB. CHOICES:** 1

6 servings

Balsamic Chicken

12 boneless skinless chicken thighs (about 1 1/2 lb)

1/2 cup white wine or apple juice

1/2 cup chicken broth

2 tablespoons lemon juice

2 tablespoons balsamic or red wine vinegar

1 tablespoon chopped fresh or 1/2 teaspoon dried thyme leaves

2 teaspoons grated lemon peel

1 teaspoon paprika

1/2 teaspoon salt

1/4 teaspoon pepper

Total Carbs **1g**
Net Carbs **1g**

prep time:
30 minutes

start to finish:
**2 hours
50 minutes**

1 Remove fat from chicken. In shallow glass or plastic dish, mix remaining ingredients. Add chicken; turn to coat. Cover and refrigerate at least 2 hours but no longer than 24 hours.

2 In 12-inch nonstick skillet, place chicken and marinade. Heat to boiling; reduce heat. Cover and simmer 15 to 20 minutes or until juice of chicken is no longer pink when centers of thickest pieces are cut. Remove chicken; keep warm.

3 Heat marinade to boiling. Boil about 6 minutes or until liquid is reduced by half. Pour over chicken.

1 serving: Cal. 190 (Cal. from Fat 80); Fat 9g (Sat. fat 3g); Chol. 70mg; Sodium 350mg; Net Carbohydrate 1g; Carbs. 1g (Fiber 0g); Pro. 24g | **% daily value:** Vit. A 6%; Vit. C 2%; Calc. 4%; Iron 15% | **exchanges:** 3 1/2 Lean Meat | **CARB. CHOICES:** 0

Total Carbs **14g**
Net Carbs **11g**

prep time:
30 minutes

start to finish:
30 minutes

4 servings

Chicken and Strawberry-Spinach Salad

3 tablespoons apple juice

2 tablespoons strawberry spreadable fruit

2 tablespoons balsamic vinegar

1 lb boneless skinless chicken breast halves

8 cups bite-size pieces spinach

1 cup strawberries, stems removed, cut in half

1/4 cup crumbled Gorgonzola cheese (1 oz)

2 tablespoons finely chopped walnuts

1 In small bowl, mix apple juice, spreadable fruit and vinegar until blended.

2 Spray 8- or 10-inch skillet with cooking spray; heat over medium-high heat. Cook chicken in skillet 15 to 20 minutes, turning once, until juice of chicken is no longer pink when centers of thickest pieces are cut. Remove chicken to cutting board. Add strawberry dressing mixture to skillet; stir to loosen any chicken drippings.

3 Cut chicken into slices. Arrange spinach on individual serving plates. Top with chicken, strawberry halves and cheese. Drizzle with strawberry dressing mixture. Sprinkle with walnuts.

1 serving: Cal. 240 (Cal. from Fat 80); Fat 8g (Sat. fat 2.5g); Chol. 75mg; Sodium 210mg; Net Carbohydrate 11g; Carbs. 14g (Fiber 3g); Pro. 29g | **% daily value:** Vit. A 110%; Vit. C 60%; Calc. 10%; Iron 15% | **exchanges:** 1/2 Starch, 1/2 Other Carb., 4 Very Lean Meat, 1 Fat | **CARB. CHOICES:** 1

Chicken and Strawberry-Spinach Salad

Chicken with Savory Sauce

prep time:
40 minutes

start to finish:
**1 hour
10 minutes**

carb-bit

This tasty recipe is also known as *pollo ubriaco* ("drunken chicken"); sometimes 2 full cups of wine (1 white and 1 red) are added, twice what we have here. In this recipe the vinegar offers the contrast in flavor instead of red wine, and the currants bring a sweet note to the peppery undertone. Try serving with whole wheat spaghetti.

1 tablespoon olive or vegetable oil

4 medium green onions, sliced (1/4 cup)

2 tablespoons chopped fresh rosemary leaves

2 tablespoons chopped fresh parsley

2 teaspoons chopped fresh thyme leaves

2 cloves garlic, finely chopped

1 red jalapeño chile, seeded, finely chopped

6 boneless skinless chicken thighs or 4 boneless skinless chicken breast halves (about 1 1/4 lb)

1 cup sliced shiitake or regular white mushrooms (3 oz)

1 cup dry white wine or chicken broth

1 tablespoon balsamic vinegar

1 tablespoon currants

1/2 teaspoon salt

1 In 12-inch nonstick skillet, heat oil over medium heat. Cook onions, rosemary, parsley, thyme, garlic and chili in oil 5 minutes, stirring frequently.

2 Add chicken to skillet. Cook about 15 minutes, turning occasionally, until chicken is brown. Add mushrooms, 1/2 cup of the wine and the vinegar. Heat to boiling; reduce heat. Simmer uncovered about 5 minutes or until about half of the liquid has evaporated.

3 Pour remaining 1/2 cup wine over chicken; sprinkle with currants and salt. Cover and simmer about 20 minutes or until juice of chicken is no longer pink when centers of thickest pieces are cut. Uncover and cook 5 minutes longer to crisp chicken.

1 serving: Cal. 270 (Cal. from Fat 130); Fat 15g (Sat. fat 4g); Chol. 90mg; Sodium 380mg; Net Carbohydrate 4g; Carbs. 4g (Fiber 0g); Pro. 31g | **% daily value:** Vit. A 8%; Vit. C 6%; Calc. 6%; Iron 20% | **exchanges:** 4 1/2 Lean Meat, 1/2 Fat | **CARB. CHOICES:** 0

Chicken with Savory Sauce

Crunchy Herbed Baked Chicken Breasts

6 boneless skinless chicken breast halves (about 1 3/4 lb)	2 teaspoons chopped fresh or 1/2 teaspoon dried rosemary leaves
1/2 cup fat-free mayonnaise or salad dressing	2 teaspoons chopped fresh or 1/2 teaspoon dried thyme leaves
1 teaspoon garlic salt	1 cup cornflakes cereal, crushed (1/2 cup)
1 tablespoon chopped fresh or 1 teaspoon dried marjoram leaves	1/2 teaspoon paprika

1 Heat oven to 375°F. Spray 13×9-inch pan with cooking spray. Remove fat from chicken.

2 In small bowl, mix mayonnaise, garlic salt, marjoram, rosemary and thyme. In shallow dish, mix cereal and paprika. Spread rounded tablespoon of mayonnaise mixture over both sides of each chicken breast half; coat evenly with cereal mixture. Place chicken in pan.

3 Bake uncovered 30 to 35 minutes or until juice of chicken is no longer pink when centers of thickest pieces are cut.

Total Carbs **7g**
Net Carbs **7g**

prep time:
15 minutes

start to finish:
50 minutes

carb-bit

Serve with fresh asparagus spears sprinkled with chopped roasted red bell peppers (from 7-ounce jar) and a little grated lemon peel.

---

1 serving: Cal. 190 (Cal. from Fat 45); Fat 5g (Sat. fat 1.5g); Chol. 80mg; Sodium 430mg; Net Carbohydrate 7g; Carbs. 7g (Fiber 0g); Pro. 29g | **% daily value:** Vit. A 6%; Vit. C 0%; Calc. 2%; Iron 15% | **exchanges:** 1/2 Other Carb., 4 Very Lean Meat, 1/2 Fat | **CARB. CHOICES:** 1/2

4 servings

Baked Oregano Chicken

Total Carbs **7g**
Net Carbs **7g**

4 boneless skinless chicken breast halves (about 1 1/4 lb)

1/4 cup dry bread crumbs

2 tablespoons grated Parmesan cheese

1/4 teaspoon dried oregano leaves

1/8 teaspoon garlic salt

1/8 teaspoon pepper

1/4 cup Dijon mustard

prep time:
10 minutes

start to finish:
35 minutes

1 Heat oven to 425°F. Spray 9-inch square pan with cooking spray. Remove fat from chicken.

2 In shallow dish, mix bread crumbs, cheese, oregano, garlic salt and pepper. Spread mustard on all sides of chicken. Coat chicken with bread crumb mixture. Place in pan.

3 Bake uncovered about 25 minutes or until juice of chicken is no longer pink when centers of thickest pieces are cut.

carb-bit

Serve this Parmesan-spiked chicken with hot cooked fresh whole green beans tossed with halved grape tomatoes, olive oil and garlic salt to taste. Heat just until tomatoes are hot.

1 serving: Cal. 220 (Cal. from Fat 60); Fat 7g (Sat. fat 2g); Chol. 90mg; Sodium 640mg; Net Carbohydrate 7g; Carbs. 7g (Fiber 0g); Pro. 34g | **% daily value:** Vit. A 0%; Vit. C 0%; Calc. 8%; Iron 10% | **exchanges:** 1/2 Starch, 4 1/2 Very Lean Meat, 1/2 Fat | **CARB. CHOICES:** 1/2

Crunchy Garlic Chicken

Total Carbs **9g**
Net Carbs **9g**

prep time:
15 minutes

start to finish:
40 minutes

6 boneless skinless chicken breast halves (about 1 3/4 lb)

3 tablespoons butter or margarine, melted

1 tablespoon fat-free (skim) milk

1 tablespoon chopped fresh chives or parsley

1/2 teaspoon salt

1/2 teaspoon garlic powder

2 cups cornflakes, crushed (1 cup)

3 tablespoons chopped fresh parsley

1/2 teaspoon paprika

Cooking spray

1 Heat oven to 425°F. Spray 13×9-inch pan with cooking spray. Remove fat from chicken. In small bowl, mix butter, milk, chives, salt and garlic powder. In shallow dish, mix cornflakes, parsley and paprika.

2 Dip chicken into butter mixture, then coat lightly and evenly with cornflakes mixture. Place in pan. Spray chicken with cooking spray.

3 Bake uncovered 20 to 25 minutes or until juice of chicken is no longer pink when centers of thickest pieces are cut.

1 serving: Cal. 240 (Cal. from Fat 90); Fat 10g (Sat. fat 4g); Chol. 95mg; Sodium 380mg; Net Carbohydrate 9g; Carbs. 9g (Fiber 0g); Pro. 30g | **% daily value:** Vit. A 15%; Vit. C 4%; Calc. 2%; Iron 20% | **exchanges:** 1/2 Starch, 4 Very Lean Meat, 1 1/2 Fat | **CARB. CHOICES:** 1/2

6 servings

Oven-Fried Chicken Nuggets

2 lb boneless skinless chicken breast halves

3/4 cup cornflakes cereal

1/2 cup all-purpose flour

3/4 teaspoon salt

1/2 teaspoon paprika

1/2 teaspoon pepper

1/3 cup buttermilk

Cooking spray

1 Heat oven to 400°F. Line 15×10×1-inch pan with foil. Remove fat from chicken. Cut chicken into 2-inch pieces.

2 In blender, place cereal, flour, salt, paprika and pepper. Cover and blend on medium speed until cereal is reduced to crumbs; pour into bowl.

3 In heavy-duty resealable plastic food-storage bag, place chicken and buttermilk. Seal bag and let stand 5 minutes, turning once. Dip chicken into cereal mixture to coat. Place in pan. Spray chicken with cooking spray.

4 Bake uncovered about 30 minutes or until crisp and chicken is no longer pink in center.

Total Carbs **12g**
Net Carbs **12g**

prep time:
20 minutes

start to finish:
50 minutes

carb-bit

You won't believe these crunchy, tasty chicken bites are baked in a light cornflake crust instead of a heavy, greasy breading. Serve with your favorite dipping sauces, but keep in mind they can add extra calories and carbs.

1 serving: Cal. 230 (Cal. from Fat 45); Fat 5g (Sat. fat 1.5g); Chol. 90mg; Sodium 410mg; Net Carbohydrate 12g; Carbs. 12g (Fiber 0g); Pro. 35g | **% daily value:** Vit. A 4%; Vit. C 0%; Calc. 4%; Iron 15% | **exchanges:** 1/2 Starch, 4 1/2 Very Lean Meat, 1/2 Fat | **CARB. CHOICES:** 1

6 servings

Thai Chicken with Cucumber-Red Onion Relish

prep time:
25 minutes

start to finish:
40 minutes

1/4 cup water

1/2 cup lime juice

1/2 cup reduced-sodium soy sauce

2 serrano or jalapeño chilies, seeded, finely chopped

2 tablespoons sugar

2 cups chopped peeled cucumber

1 small red onion, cut lengthwise in half, then cut crosswise into thin slices

6 boneless skinless chicken breast halves (about 1 3/4 lb)

1 In blender or food processor, place water, 1/4 cup of the lime juice, 1/4 cup of the soy sauce, the chilies and sugar. Cover and blend on high speed about 1 minute or until blended. In shallow dish, place cucumber and onion; add blended mixture. Cover and refrigerate until serving.

2 Remove fat from chicken. In shallow glass or plastic dish or resealable plastic food-storage bag, mix remaining 1/4 cup lime juice and 1/4 cup soy sauce. Add chicken; turn to coat. Cover dish or seal bag and refrigerate 15 minutes.

3 Set oven control to broil. Spray broiler pan rack with cooking spray. Remove chicken from marinade; reserve marinade. Place chicken on rack in broiler pan. Brush chicken with marinade. Broil chicken with tops 5 to 7 inches from heat 7 minutes. Turn chicken; brush with marinade. Broil about 7 minutes longer or until juice of chicken is no longer pink when centers of thickest pieces are cut. Discard any remaining marinade. Serve chicken with cucumber relish.

1 serving: Cal. 200 (Cal. from Fat 40); Fat 4.5g (Sat. fat 1g); Chol. 80mg; Sodium 790mg; Net Carbohydrate 10g; Carbs. 10g (Fiber 0g); Pro. 31g | **% daily value:** Vit. A 2%; Vit. C 8%; Calc. 2%; Iron 8% | **exchanges:** 1/2 Other Carb., 1/2 Vegetable, 4 Very Lean Meat, 1/2 Fat | **CARB. CHOICES:** 1/2

4 servings

Fiesta Chicken and Rice

1 1/4 cups water

1 can (5.5 oz) spicy eight-vegetable juice

1 package (4.9 oz) rice and vermicelli mix with chicken broth and broccoli

1 1/2 cups cubed cooked chicken or turkey

1 cup frozen stir-fry bell peppers and onions (from 1-lb bag), thawed

1 In 3-quart saucepan, heat water, vegetable juice and rice-vermicelli mix with seasoning packet to boiling, stirring occasionally; reduce heat.

2 Cover and simmer 15 to 20 minutes, stirring occasionally. Stir in chicken and stir-fry vegetables; heat through.

Total Carbs **14g**
Net Carbs **14g**

prep time:
35 minutes

start to finish:
35 minutes

1 serving: Cal. 160 (Cal. from Fat 35); Fat 4g (Sat. fat 1g); Chol. 45mg; Sodium 290mg; Net Carbohydrate 14g; Carbs. 14g (Fiber 0g); Pro. 17g | **% daily value:** Vit. A 15%; Vit. C 20%; Calc. 2%; Iron 8% | **exchanges:** 1 Starch, 2 Lean Meat | **CARB. CHOICES:** 1

Total Carbs **8g**
Net Carbs **6g**

prep time:
20 minutes

start to finish:
20 minutes

6 servings

Southwestern Chicken BLT Salad

1/2 cup thick 'n chunky salsa

1/2 cup refrigerated bacon-flavored dip

1 tablespoon chopped fresh parsley

1 bag (10 oz) romaine and leaf lettuce mix

2 packages (6 oz each) refrigerated cooked Southwest-flavor chicken breast strips

4 roma (plum) tomatoes, coarsely chopped

1/2 cup chopped cooked bacon

1/2 cup croutons

1 In small bowl, mix salsa, dip and parsley.

2 In large bowl, mix remaining ingredients. Add salsa mixture; toss until coated.

1 serving: Cal. 190 (Cal. from Fat 90); Fat 10g (Sat. fat 4g); Chol. 50mg; Sodium 730mg; Net Carbohydrate 6g; Carbs. 8g (Fiber 2g); Pro. 16g | **% daily value:** Vit. A 40%; Vit. C 25%; Calc. 4%; Iron 6% | **exchanges:** 1/2 Starch, 2 Very Lean Meat, 2 Fat | **CARB. CHOICES:** 1/2

4 servings

Turkey Tenderloins and Mixed Sweet Peppers

Total Carbs **9g**
Net Carbs **8g**

prep time:
30 minutes

start to finish:
30 minutes

1 lb turkey breast tenderloins

3 medium red, yellow, orange or green bell peppers, cut into 1/4-inch strips

2/3 cup chicken broth

1 teaspoon dried basil leaves

1/4 teaspoon salt

1/4 teaspoon ground red pepper (cayenne)

3 tablespoons white wine vinegar

1 tablespoon cornstarch

1 Heat 10-inch nonstick skillet over medium heat. Cook turkey in skillet about 5 minutes, turning once, until brown. Remove turkey from skillet.

2 Add bell peppers to skillet. Cook over medium heat about 3 minutes, stirring frequently, until crisp-tender. Stir in broth, basil, salt and red pepper. Heat to boiling; reduce heat. Return turkey to skillet. Cover and simmer about 10 minutes, stirring occasionally, until juice of turkey is no longer pink when centers of thickest pieces are cut.

3 Remove turkey from skillet; keep warm. Push bell peppers from center of skillet. In small bowl, mix vinegar and cornstarch; stir into liquid in skillet. Heat to boiling, stirring constantly. Boil and stir 1 minute. Stir peppers into sauce to coat. Cut turkey into thin slices. Serve turkey with sauce.

1 serving: Cal. 160 (Cal. from Fat 15); Fat 1.5g (Sat. fat 0g); Chol. 75mg; Sodium 370mg; Net Carbohydrate 8g; Carbs. 9g (Fiber 1g); Pro. 28g | **% daily value:** Vit. A 40%; Vit. C 110%; Calc. 2%; Iron 10% | **exchanges:** 1 Vegetable, 3 1/2 Very Lean Meat | **CARB. CHOICES:** 1/2

Total Carbs **16g**
Net Carbs **14g**

prep time:
25 minutes

start to finish:
25 minutes

6 servings

California-Style Turkey Patties with Corn and Tomato Relish

Corn and Tomato Relish

1 can (11 oz) whole kernel corn with red and green peppers, drained

2 medium stalks celery, sliced (1 cup)

12 cherry tomatoes, cut into fourths

2 tablespoons lemon juice

Turkey Patties

1 1/2 lb ground turkey breast

1 medium onion, chopped (1/2 cup)

1 cup soft bread crumbs (about 1 1/2 slices bread)

1/2 teaspoon salt

1/4 teaspoon pepper

1/3 cup chicken broth

1 In medium bowl, mix all relish ingredients; set aside.

2 In large bowl, mix remaining ingredients. Shape mixture into 6 patties, each about 1/2 inch thick.

3 Set oven control to broil. Spray broiler pan rack with cooking spray. Place patties on rack in broiler pan. Broil with tops 4 inches from heat about 12 minutes, turning once, until no longer pink in center. Serve patties with relish.

1 serving: Cal. 190 (Cal. from Fat 15); Fat 1.5g (Sat. fat 0g); Chol. 75mg; Sodium 360mg; Net Carbohydrate 14g; Carbs. 16g (Fiber 2g); Pro. 29g | **% daily value:** Vit. A 8%; Vit. C 15%; Calc. 4%; Iron 10% | **exchanges:** 1 Starch, 3 1/2 Very Lean Meat | **CARB. CHOICES:** 1

California-Style Turkey Patties with Corn and Tomato Relish

Total Carbs **10g**
Net Carbs **7g**

prep time:
15 minutes

start to finish:
30 minutes

4 servings

Honey-Mustard Turkey with Snap Peas

1 lb uncooked turkey breast slices, about 1/4 inch thick

1/2 cup Dijon and honey marinade

1 cup baby-cut carrots, cut lengthwise in half

2 cups frozen snap pea pods (from 1-lb bag)

1 In shallow glass or plastic dish, place turkey. Pour marinade over turkey; turn slices to coat evenly. Cover dish and let stand 10 minutes at room temperature.

2 Spray 10-inch skillet with cooking spray; heat over medium heat. Drain most of marinade from turkey. Cook turkey in skillet about 5 minutes, turning once, until brown.

3 Add carrots, lifting turkey to place carrots on bottom of skillet. Top turkey with pea pods. Cover and simmer about 7 minutes or until carrots are tender and turkey is no longer pink in center.

1 serving: Cal. 200 (Cal. from Fat 50); Fat 6g (Sat. fat 1g); Chol. 75mg; Sodium 210mg; Net Carbohydrate 7g; Carbs. 10g (Fiber 3g); Pro. 29g | **% daily value:** Vit. A 120%; Vit. C 30%; Calc. 6%; Iron 15% | **exchanges:** 1 Vegetable, 4 Very Lean Meat, 1 Fat | **CARB. CHOICES:** 1/2

5 Fish and Seafood

Gremolata-Topped Sea Bass   148

Lemon-Garlic Halibut Steaks   150

Broiled Salmon with Orange-Mustard
  Glaze   152

Orange and Dill Pan-Seared Tuna   153

Marinated Tuna Steaks with Cucumber
  Sauce   154

Red Snapper with Mango Salsa   155

Grilled Creole Snapper   156

Cornmeal-Crusted Catfish   157

Grilled Fish Tacos   158

Parmesan Perch   160

Grilled Shrimp Kabobs   161

Southwestern Stir-Fried Shrimp   162

Savory Shrimp and Scallops   164

Whitefish and Shrimp Cakes   166

Spinach-Shrimp Salad with Hot Bacon
  Dressing   168

◖ = **super express** ready in 30 minutes or less

Total Carbs **6g**
Net Carbs **6g**

prep time:
5 minutes

start to finish:
25 minutes

carb-bit

Lemon juice and lemon peel contribute tons of flavor but few carbs; 1 tablespoon lemon juice has only about 1.5 grams.

4 servings

Gremolata-Topped Sea Bass

1/4 cup Italian-style dry bread crumbs

1/4 cup chopped fresh parsley

2 teaspoons grated lemon peel

1 tablespoon butter or margarine, melted

1 lb sea bass, mahimahi or other medium-firm fish fillets

1/4 teaspoon seasoned salt

1 tablespoon lemon juice

1 Heat oven to 425°F. Line 13×9-inch pan with foil; spray foil with cooking spray. In small bowl, mix bread crumbs, parsley, lemon peel and butter.

2 Cut fish into 4 serving pieces. Place fish in pan. Sprinkle with seasoned salt. Drizzle with lemon juice. Spoon crumb mixture over each piece; press lightly.

3 Bake uncovered 15 to 20 minutes or until fish flakes easily with a fork.

1 serving: Cal. 190 (Cal. from Fat 80); Fat 9g (Sat. fat 3g); Chol. 70mg; Sodium 220mg; Net Carbohydrate 6g; Carbs. 6g (Fiber 0g); Pro. 22g | **% daily value:** Vit. A 10%; Vit. C 8%; Calc. 4%; Iron 8% | **exchanges:** 1/2 Starch, 3 Very Lean Meat, 1 1/2 Fat | **CARB. CHOICES:** 1/2

Gremolata-Topped Sea Bass

super express

Total Carbs **2g**
Net Carbs **2g**

prep time:
20 minutes

start to finish:
30 minutes

4 servings

Lemon-Garlic Halibut Steaks

1/4 cup lemon juice

I tablespoon olive or vegetable oil

1/4 teaspoon salt

1/4 teaspoon pepper

2 cloves garlic, finely chopped

4 halibut or tuna steaks, about I inch thick (about 2 lb)

1/4 cup chopped fresh parsley

I tablespoon grated lemon peel

1   Brush grill rack with vegetable oil. Heat coals or gas grill for direct heat. In shallow glass or plastic dish or resealable plastic food-storage bag, mix lemon juice, oil, salt, pepper and garlic. Add fish; turn several times to coat. Cover dish or seal bag and refrigerate 10 minutes.

2   Remove fish from marinade; reserve marinade. Cover and grill fish over medium heat 10 to 15 minutes, turning once and brushing with marinade, until fish flakes easily with a fork. Discard any remaining marinade.

3   Sprinkle fish with parsley and lemon peel.

I serving: Cal. 240 (Cal. from Fat 60); Fat 6g (Sat. fat 1g); Chol. 120mg; Sodium 340mg; Net Carbohydrate 2g; Carbs. 2g (Fiber 0g); Pro. 43g | **% daily value:** Vit. A 8%; Vit. C 10%; Calc. 4%; Iron 6% | **exchanges:** 7 Very Lean Meat | **CARB. CHOICES:** 0

Lemon-Garlic Halibut Steaks

Total Carbs **7g**
Net Carbs **7g**

prep time:
5 minutes

start to finish:
20 minutes

4 servings

Broiled Salmon with Orange-Mustard Glaze

1 lb salmon fillet, 1/2 inch thick

2 tablespoons orange marmalade

2 teaspoons mustard seed

1/4 teaspoon salt

1/8 teaspoon red pepper sauce

1 Set oven control to broil. Spray broiler pan rack with cooking spray. Cut salmon crosswise into 4 pieces. Place salmon, skin side down, on rack in broiler pan. Broil with tops 4 inches from heat 10 to 15 minutes or until fish flakes easily with fork.

2 Meanwhile, in small bowl, mix remaining ingredients. Spread on salmon during last 5 minutes of broiling.

1 serving: Cal. 190 (Cal. from Fat 60); Fat 7g (Sat. fat 2g); Chol. 75mg; Sodium 220mg; Net Carbohydrate 7g; Carbs. 7g (Fiber 0g); Pro. 25g | **% daily value:** Vit. A 2%; Vit. C 2%; Calc. 2%; Iron 6% | **exchanges:** 1/2 Other Carb., 3 1/2 Very Lean Meat, 1 Fat | **CARB. CHOICES:** 1/2

4 servings

Orange and Dill Pan-Seared Tuna

Total Carbs **7g**
Net Carbs **7g**

prep time:
20 minutes

start to finish:
20 minutes

4 tuna, swordfish or other firm fish steaks, 3/4 inch thick (4 oz each)

1/2 teaspoon peppered seasoned salt

1 small red onion, thinly sliced (1/2 cup)

3/4 cup orange juice

1 tablespoon chopped fresh or 1/4 teaspoon dried dill weed

1 tablespoon butter or margarine

1 teaspoon grated orange peel, if desired

1 Heat 10-inch nonstick skillet over medium-high heat. Sprinkle both sides of fish with peppered seasoned salt. Add fish to skillet; reduce heat to medium-low. Cover and cook 6 to 8 minutes, turning once, until edges of tuna are opaque and center is slightly translucent. (If using swordfish, cook until fish flakes easily with fork.) Remove fish from skillet; keep warm.

2 Add onion to skillet. Cook over medium-high heat 2 minutes, stirring occasionally. Stir in orange juice; cook 2 minutes. Stir in dill weed, butter and orange peel. Cook 1 to 2 minutes or until slightly thickened. Serve sauce over fish.

1 serving: Cal. 190 (Cal. from Fat 80); Fat 9g (Sat. fat 3g); Chol. 75mg; Sodium 250mg; Net Carbohydrate 7g; Carbs. 7g (Fiber 0g); Pro. 22g | **% daily value:** Vit. A 6%; Vit. C 20%; Calc. 2%; Iron 4% | **exchanges:** 1/2 Other Carb., 3 Very Lean Meat, 1 1/2 Fat | **CARB. CHOICES:** 1/2

Marinated Tuna Steaks with Cucumber Sauce

3 tablespoons lime juice

1/4 cup chopped fresh cilantro

1 clove garlic, finely chopped

1/4 teaspoon salt

1 lb tuna steaks

1/2 cup chopped cucumber

1/4 cup plain yogurt

1 tablespoon fat-free mayonnaise or salad dressing

1 In 9-inch glass pie plate, mix lime juice, 2 tablespoons of the cilantro, the garlic and salt. Cut tuna steaks into 4 serving pieces. Add tuna to lime mixture, turning several times to coat. Cover and refrigerate 1 hour, turning once.

2 Meanwhile, in small bowl, mix cucumber, yogurt, mayonnaise and remaining 2 tablespoons cilantro; cover and refrigerate.

3 Set oven control to boil. Spray broiler pan rack with cooking spray. Remove tuna from marinade; discard marinade. Place tuna on rack in broiler pan. Broil with tops 4 inches from heat 7 to 10 minutes, turning once, until tuna flakes easily with fork. Serve with cucumber sauce.

Total Carbs 3g
Net Carbs 3g

prep time:
20 minutes

start to finish:
**1 hour
20 minutes**

carb-bit

Oh, those wonderful cukes! Cool, crunchy, fat free and only about 2 carbs for a half cup of slices.

1 serving: Cal. 160 (Cal. from Fat 60); Fat 6g (Sat. fat 2g); Chol. 70mg; Sodium 250mg; Net Carbohydrate 3g; Carbs. 3g (Fiber 0g); Pro. 23g | **% daily value:** Vit. A 4%; Vit. C 4%; Calc. 4%; Iron 4% | **exchanges:** 3 1/2 Very Lean Meat, 1 Fat | **CARB. CHOICES:** 0

Red Snapper with Mango Salsa

1 small mango, cut lengthwise in half, seed removed and diced (3/4 cup)

1 small tomato, diced (1/2 cup)

2 tablespoons finely chopped red onion

1/2 cup chopped fresh cilantro

1/4 cup lime juice

1 lb red snapper, orange roughy or walleye fillets

Cooking spray

1/2 teaspoon salt

1 In small glass or plastic bowl, mix mango, tomato, onion, cilantro and lime juice. Cover and let stand 30 minutes.

2 Set oven control to broil. Place fish on rack in broiler pan. Spray fish with cooking spray; sprinkle with salt. Broil with tops 4 to 6 inches from heat 5 to 8 minutes or until fish is light brown and flakes easily with fork. Serve with mango salsa.

Total Carbs **11g**	
Net Carbs **10g**	

prep time:
20 minutes

start to finish:
50 minutes

1 serving: Cal. 140 (Cal. from Fat 15); Fat 1.5g (Sat. fat 0g); Chol. 60mg; Sodium 390mg; Net Carbohydrate 10g; Carbs. 11g (Fiber 1g); Pro. 22g | **% daily value:** Vit. A 15%; Vit. C 20%; Calc. 2%; Iron 4% | **exchanges:** 1/2 Fruit, 3 Very Lean Meat | **CARB. CHOICES:** 1

super express

prep time:
30 minutes

start to finish:
30 minutes

carb-bit

The chunky topping of grilled veggies for these southern-spiced fillets makes this a perfect summertime dish. For a crisp and cooling sidekick, skip the rice and toss together a salad of leafy greens, celery, cukes and sliced fresh tomatoes.

4 servings

Grilled Creole Snapper

2 medium tomatoes, cut crosswise in half

1 medium onion, cut into fourths

1/2 medium green bell pepper, cut in half

4 medium green onions, thinly sliced (1/4 cup)

1 1/2 tablespoons red wine vinegar

1/2 teaspoon dried thyme leaves

1/2 teaspoon salt

1/4 teaspoon red pepper sauce

1 1/2 lb red snapper, sole or flounder fillets, about 1/2 inch thick

Cooking spray

2 tablespoons chopped fresh parsley

Hot cooked brown rice, if desired

1. Heat coals or gas grill for direct heat. Spray large piece of heavy-duty foil with cooking spray. Place tomatoes, onion and bell pepper on foil. Wrap foil securely around vegetables. Cover and grill foil packet, seam sides up, over medium heat 6 minutes, turning once.

2. Meanwhile, in large bowl, mix green onions, vinegar, thyme, salt and pepper sauce; set aside.

3. Spray fish and hinged wire grill basket with cooking spray. Place fish in basket. Cover and grill fish 7 to 8 minutes, turning once, until fish flakes easily with fork.

4. Place fish on serving platter; keep warm. Coarsely chop grilled vegetables. Toss vegetables, parsley and green onion mixture; spoon over fish. Serve with rice.

1 serving: Cal. 180 (Cal. from Fat 20); Fat 2.5g (Sat. fat 0.5g); Chol. 90mg; Sodium 440mg; Net Carbohydrate 7g; Carbs. 7g (Fiber 2g); Pro. 33g | **% daily value:** Vit. A 15%; Vit. C 25%; Calc. 4%; Iron 6% | **exchanges:** 1 Vegetable, 4 1/2 Very Lean Meat | **CARB. CHOICES:** 1/2

4 servings

Cornmeal-Crusted Catfish

1/4 cup yellow cornmeal

1/4 cup dry bread crumbs

1 teaspoon chili powder

1/2 teaspoon paprika

1/2 teaspoon garlic salt

1/4 teaspoon pepper

1 lb catfish fillets, about 3/4 inch thick

1/4 cup fat-free ranch dressing

Chopped fresh parsley, if desired

Total Carbs **16g**
Net Carbs **16g**

prep time:
10 minutes

start to finish:
25 minutes

1 Heat oven to 450°F. Spray broiler pan rack with cooking spray. In shallow dish, mix cornmeal, bread crumbs, chili powder, paprika, garlic salt and pepper.

2 Remove and discard skin from fish. Cut fish into 4 serving pieces. Lightly brush dressing on all sides of fish. Coat fish with cornmeal mixture. Place fish on rack in broiler pan.

3 Bake uncovered about 15 minutes or until fish flakes easily with fork. Sprinkle with parsley.

1 serving: Cal. 240 (Cal. from Fat 70); Fat 8g (Sat. fat 1.5g); Chol. 85mg; Sodium 370mg; Net Carbohydrate 16g; Carbs. 16g (Fiber 0g); Pro. 25g | **% daily value:** Vit. A 10%; Vit. C 0%; Calc. 8%; Iron 15% | **exchanges:** 1 Starch, 3 Lean Meat | **CARB. CHOICES:** 1

Total Carbs **13g**
Net Carbs **11g**

prep time:
20 minutes

start to finish:
20 minutes

8 tacos

Grilled Fish Tacos

I lb firm white fish fillets, such as sea bass, red snapper or halibut

I tablespoon olive or vegetable oil

I teaspoon ground cumin or chili powder

I/2 teaspoon salt

I/4 teaspoon pepper

8 corn tortillas (6 inch)

I/4 cup sour cream

Toppers (shredded lettuce, chopped avocado, chopped tomatoes, chopped onion and chopped fresh cilantro), if desired

I/2 cup salsa

1 Brush grill rack with vegetable oil. Heat coals or gas grill for direct heat.

2 Brush fish with oil; sprinkle with cumin, salt and pepper. Cover and grill fish over medium heat 5 to 7 minutes, turning once, until fish flakes easily with a fork.

3 Heat tortillas as directed on package. Spread sour cream on tortillas. Add fish, toppers and salsa.

I taco: Cal. 150 (Cal. from Fat 60); Fat 7g (Sat. fat 2g); Chol. 35mg; Sodium 290mg; Net Carbohydrate 11g; Carbs. 13g (Fiber 2g); Pro. 12g | **% daily value:** Vit. A 4%; Vit. C 2%; Calc. 6%; Iron 6% | **exchanges:** I Starch, I Very Lean Meat, I Fat | **CARB. CHOICES:** I

Grilled Fish Tacos

Total Carbs **3g**
Net Carbs **3g**

prep time:
10 minutes

start to finish:
20 minutes

4 servings

Parmesan Perch

I lb ocean perch, cod or haddock fillets

2 tablespoons dry bread crumbs

I tablespoon grated Parmesan cheese

I teaspoon dried basil leaves

1/2 teaspoon paprika

Dash of pepper

I tablespoon butter or margarine, melted

2 tablespoons chopped fresh parsley

1 Move oven rack to position slightly above middle of oven. Heat oven to 500°F. Spray 13×9-inch pan with cooking spray.

2 If fish fillets are large, cut into 4 serving pieces. In shallow dish, mix bread crumbs, cheese, basil, paprika and pepper. Brush one side of each piece of fish with butter; dip into crumb mixture. Place fish, coated sides up, in pan.

3 Bake uncovered about 10 minutes or until fish flakes easily with fork. Sprinkle with parsley.

I serving: Cal. 150 (Cal. from Fat 45); Fat 5g (Sat. fat 2g); Chol. 70mg; Sodium 170mg; Net Carbohydrate 3g; Carbs. 3g (Fiber 0g); Pro. 23g | **% daily value:** Vit. A 10%; Vit. C 2%; Calc. 6%; Iron 4% | **exchanges:** 3 1/2 Very Lean Meat, 1/2 Fat | **CARB. CHOICES:** 0

4 servings

Grilled Shrimp Kabobs

1 lb uncooked peeled deveined large shrimp, thawed if frozen and tails peeled

1 cup fat-free Italian dressing

1 medium red onion, cut into 8 pieces

1 medium bell pepper, cut into 8 pieces

16 medium cherry tomatoes

16 small whole mushrooms

Total Carbs **15g**
Net Carbs **12g**

prep time:
20 minutes

start to finish:
50 minutes

1 In shallow glass or plastic dish or heavy-duty resealable plastic food-storage bag, place shrimp and dressing. Cover dish or seal bag and refrigerate 30 minutes.

2 Heat coals or gas grill for direct heat. Remove shrimp from marinade; reserve marinade. On each of four 15-inch metal skewers, thread shrimp, onion, bell pepper, tomatoes and mushrooms alternately, leaving 1/4-inch space between each piece.

3 Cover and grill kabobs over medium heat 6 to 8 minutes, turning frequently and brushing several times with marinade, until shrimp are pink and firm. Discard any remaining marinade.

1 serving: Cal. 150 (Cal. from Fat 20); Fat 2g (Sat. fat 0g); Chol. 165mg; Sodium 850mg; Net Carbohydrate 12g; Carbs. 15g (Fiber 3g); Pro. 21g | **% daily value:** Vit. A 20%; Vit. C 40%; Calc. 6%; Iron 20% | **exchanges:** 1/2 Other Carb., 1 Vegetable, 2 1/2 Very Lean Meat | **CARB. CHOICES:** 1

Southwestern Stir-Fried Shrimp

prep time:
20 minutes

start to finish:
1 hour
20 minutes

carb-bit

Keep the southwest flavor by serving with steamed fresh broccoli spears sprinkled with a little grated lime peel.

2 tablespoons lime juice

2 teaspoons cornstarch

1/2 teaspoon ground cumin

1/4 teaspoon salt

1/4 teaspoon pepper

1 lb uncooked peeled deveined large shrimp (about 24), thawed if frozen and tails peeled

1 large yellow bell pepper, chopped (1 1/2 cups)

1 large red bell pepper, chopped (1 1/2 cups)

1 medium onion, chopped (1/2 cup)

1/3 cup chicken broth

2 cloves garlic, finely chopped

1/8 teaspoon ground red pepper (cayenne)

2 tablespoons chopped fresh cilantro

1 In medium glass or plastic bowl, mix lime juice, cornstarch, cumin, salt and pepper. Stir in shrimp. Cover and refrigerate 1 hour.

2 Heat 12-inch nonstick skillet over medium heat. Add bell peppers, onion, broth, garlic, red pepper and cilantro; cook and stir 2 minutes. Add shrimp mixture; cook and stir 3 to 4 minutes or until shrimp are pink and firm.

1 serving: Cal. 90 (Cal. from Fat 10); Fat 1g (Sat. fat 0g); Chol. 110mg; Sodium 280mg; Net Carbohydrate 7g; Carbs. 8g (Fiber 1g); Pro. 13g | **% daily value:** Vit. A 50%; Vit. C 120%; Calc. 4%; Iron 15% | **exchanges:** 1 Vegetable, 1 1/2 Very Lean Meat | **CARB. CHOICES:** 1/2

Southwestern Stir-Fried Shrimp

Savory Shrimp and Scallops

prep time:
20 minutes

start to finish:
20 minutes

carb-bit

Scallops are available in two sizes. Sea scallops are the larger of the two, about 2 inches in diameter. Bay scallops are about 1/2 inch in diameter. Both sea and bay scallops are creamy white, sweet and mild flavored. Sea scallops may be tinted light orange or pink, and bay scallops may be tinted light tan or pink. You can use whichever is available, but you may want to cut the sea scallops in half. Scallops have 0 carbs.

1 lb sea or bay scallops

2 tablespoons olive or vegetable oil

1 clove garlic, finely chopped

2 medium green onions, chopped (2 tablespoons)

1 medium green bell pepper, diced (1 cup)

1 tablespoon chopped fresh parsley or 1 teaspoon parsley flakes

1 lb uncooked peeled deveined medium shrimp, thawed if frozen and tails peeled

1/2 cup dry white wine or chicken broth

1 tablespoon fresh lemon juice

1/4 to 1/2 teaspoon crushed red pepper flakes

1 If using sea scallops, cut in half. In 10-inch skillet, heat oil over medium heat. Cook garlic, onions, bell pepper and parsley in oil about 5 minutes, stirring occasionally, until bell pepper is crisp-tender.

2 Stir in scallops and remaining ingredients. Cook 4 to 5 minutes, stirring frequently, until shrimp are pink and firm and scallops are white.

1 serving: Cal. 140 (Cal. from Fat 50); Fat 6g (Sat. fat 1g); Chol. 130mg; Sodium 230mg; Net Carbohydrate 2g; Carbs. 2g (Fiber 0g); Pro. 21g | **% daily value:** Vit. A 8%; Vit. C 20%; Calc. 8%; Iron 15% | **exchanges:** 3 Very Lean Meat, 1 Fat | **CARB. CHOICES:** 0

Savory Shrimp and Scallops

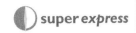
Total Carbs **2g**
Net Carbs **2g**

prep time:
30 minutes

start to finish:
30 minutes

carb-
bit

Wow, seafood, including shrimp and fish, is carb free! This take on the classic crab cake can be eaten as is or served between leaves of lettuce with reduced-fat mayonnaise, tartar sauce or salsa.

6 servings

Whitefish and Shrimp Cakes

3/4 lb whitefish, trout or catfish fillets, cut up

1/2 lb uncooked peeled deveined medium shrimp, thawed if frozen and tails peeled

4 medium green onions, chopped (1/4 cup)

2 tablespoons fat-free cholesterol-free egg product or 1 large egg white

2 tablespoons chopped fresh parsley

1 tablespoon all-purpose flour

1 tablespoon reduced-fat mayonnaise or salad dressing

1 teaspoon Dijon mustard

1/2 teaspoon salt

1/4 teaspoon pepper

1/8 teaspoon Worcestershire sauce

Reduced-fat tartar sauce or salsa, if desired

1 In food processor, place all ingredients except tartar sauce. Cover and process, using quick on-and-off motions, until fish and shrimp are coarsely chopped.

2 Heat 12-inch nonstick skillet over medium heat. Drop fish mixture by slightly less than 1/3 cupfuls into skillet; flatten with spatula. Cook 4 minutes; turn. Cook about 4 minutes longer or until patties are firm. Serve with tartar sauce.

1 serving: Cal. 120 (Cal. from Fat 45); Fat 5g (Sat. fat 1g); Chol. 85mg; Sodium 330mg; Net Carbohydrate 2g; Carbs. 2g (Fiber 0g); Pro. 18g | **% daily value:** Vit. A 6%; Vit. C 2%; Calc. 2%; Iron 10% | **exchanges:** 2 1/2 Very Lean Meat, 1 Fat | **CARB. CHOICES:** 0

Whitefish and Shrimp Cakes

Total Carbs **7g**
Net Carbs **5g**

prep time:
20 minutes

start to finish:
20 minutes

4 servings

Spinach-Shrimp Salad with Hot Bacon Dressing

3 slices bacon, cut into 1-inch pieces

1/4 cup white vinegar

1 tablespoon sugar

1/4 teaspoon ground mustard

6 cups bite-size pieces spinach leaves

1 cup sliced fresh mushrooms (3 oz)

1/4 cup crumbled feta cheese (1 oz)

1/2 lb cooked peeled deveined medium shrimp, thawed if frozen

1 In 10-inch skillet, cook bacon over medium-high heat, stirring occasionally, until crisp. Stir in vinegar, sugar and mustard; continue stirring until sugar is dissolved.

2 In large bowl, toss spinach, mushrooms, cheese and shrimp. Drizzle hot bacon dressing over spinach mixture; toss to coat. Serve immediately.

1 serving: Cal. 130 (Cal. from Fat 50); Fat 5g (Sat. fat 2.5g); Chol. 120mg; Sodium 340mg; Net Carbohydrate 5g; Carbs. 7g (Fiber 2g); Pro. 17g | **% daily value:** Vit. A 90%; Vit. C 25%; Calc. 10%; Iron 20% | **exchanges:** 1 1/2 Vegetable, 2 Very Lean Meat, 1 Fat | **CARB. CHOICES:** 1/2

6 Easy Vegetarian

Eggplant Parmesan   170

Eggplant and Gouda Cheese Pie   172

Easy Spinach Pie   173

Impossibly Easy Vegetable Pie   174

Caesar Salad Wraps   176

Family-Favorite Cheese Pizza   178

Vegetable Kung Pao   180

Savory Vegetable Stew   181

Vegetable-Rice Skillet   182

Garden Vegetable Salad   184

Cream of Broccoli Soup   185

Chunky Tomato Soup   186

Zucchini Pancakes   188

◖ = **super express** ready in 30 minutes or less

Total Carbs **18g**
Net Carbs **15g**

prep time:
30 minutes

start to finish:
30 minutes

carb-bit

**Which pasta
sauce to choose?
Chunky? Smooth?
Spicy or mild?
Pick any you like,
but check the
labels for the carb
count because
some sauces have
more sugar than
others.**

6 servings

Eggplant Parmesan

1 medium eggplant (1 1/2 lb), peeled,
cut into 1/4-inch slices

Cooking spray

1/4 cup finely shredded Parmesan cheese

1/4 cup seasoned dry bread crumbs

2 teaspoons olive or vegetable oil

1 cup tomato pasta sauce

1 1/2 cups shredded part-skim
mozzarella cheese (6 oz)

1 Set oven control to broil. Generously spray both sides of each eggplant
slice with cooking spray. Place on rack in broiler pan. Broil with tops 4
to 5 inches from heat about 10 minutes, turning once, until tender.

2 Meanwhile, in small bowl, mix Parmesan cheese and bread crumbs; toss
with oil.

3 In 1-quart saucepan, heat pasta sauce over medium heat about 2 minutes, stirring occasionally, until heated through. Remove from heat; cover
to keep warm.

4 Sprinkle 1 cup of the mozzarella cheese over eggplant slices. Spoon bread
crumb mixture over cheese. Broil about 1 minute or until cheese is
melted and crumbs are brown. Serve eggplant topped with pasta sauce
and remaining 1/2 cup mozzarella cheese.

1 serving: Cal. 200 (Cal. from Fat 90); Fat 10g (Sat. fat 5g); Chol. 20mg; Sodium 470mg; Net Carbohydrate
15g; Carbs. 18g (Fiber 3g); Pro. 11g | **% daily value:** Vit. A 10%; Vit. C 6%; Calc. 30%; Iron 6% |
exchanges: 1/2 Starch, 1 Vegetable, 1 Lean Meat, 1 1/2 Fat | **CARB. CHOICES:** 1

Eggplant Parmesan

Eggplant and Gouda Cheese Pie

2 small eggplants (about 1 lb each), peeled, cut into 3/4-inch pieces

1 cup shredded smoked Gouda cheese (4 oz)

1/2 cup ricotta cheese

1/4 cup small soft bread crumbs

1 tablespoon chopped fresh or 1 teaspoon dried basil leaves

1/2 teaspoon salt

1/8 teaspoon pepper

1 clove garlic, finely chopped

3 large eggs, beaten

1 Heat oven to 350°F. Spray 9-inch glass pie plate with cooking spray.

2 Add 1/2 inch water to saucepan or skillet; place steamer basket in saucepan (water should not touch bottom of basket). Place eggplant in steamer basket. Cover tightly and heat to boiling; reduce heat. Steam 5 to 7 minutes or until tender.

3 In large bowl, mash eggplant with fork. Stir in 3/4 cup of the Gouda cheese and the remaining ingredients. Spoon mixture into pie plate. Sprinkle with remaining 1/4 cup Gouda cheese.

4 Bake uncovered about 30 minutes or until knife inserted in center comes out clean.

Total Carbs **11g**
Net Carbs **8g**

prep time:
20 minutes

start to finish:
50 minutes

carb-bit

Eggplant adds a wonderful meaty texture to this pie but weighs in at only 3.3 grams of carbs per 1/2 cup.

---

1 serving: Cal. 170 (Cal. from Fat 90); Fat 10g (Sat. fat 5g); Chol. 135mg; Sodium 420mg; Net Carboyhdrate 8g; Carbs. 11g (Fiber 3g); Pro. 11g | **% daily value:** Vit. A 10%; Vit. C 0%; Calc. 20%; Iron 6% | **exchanges:** 1/2 Starch, 1 Vegetable, 1 High-Fat Meat, 1/2 Fat | **CARB. CHOICES:** 1

4 servings

Easy Spinach Pie

1 tablespoon butter or margarine

1 package (10 oz) washed fresh spinach, finely chopped

1 small red bell pepper, chopped (1/2 cup)

3/4 cup fat-free (skim) milk

2 tablespoons all-purpose flour

1/2 teaspoon salt

1/8 teaspoon ground nutmeg

3 large eggs

2 tablespoons grated Parmesan cheese

1 Heat oven to 350°F. Spray 9-inch glass pie plate with cooking spray.

2 In nonstick 12-inch skillet, melt butter over medium heat. Cook spinach and bell pepper in butter about 5 minutes, stirring occasionally, until spinach is wilted and bell pepper is crisp-tender.

3 In small bowl, beat remaining ingredients except cheese with fork or wire whisk until smooth; pour into skillet. Stir mixture; pour into pie plate.

4 Bake uncovered about 30 minutes or until center is set. Sprinkle with cheese. Serve immediately.

Total Carbs **9g**
Net Carbs **6g**

prep time:
20 minutes

start to finish:
50 minutes

1 serving: Cal. 140 (Cal. from Fat 70); Fat 8g (Sat. fat 3.5g); Chol. 170mg; Sodium 500mg; Net Carbohydrate 6g; Carbs. 9g (Fiber 3g); Pro. 10g | **% daily value:** Vit. A 160%; Vit. C 45%; Calc. 20%; Iron 15% | **exchanges:** 1 Vegetable, 1 Medium-Fat Meat, 1 Fat | **CARB. CHOICES:** 1/2

Impossibly Easy Vegetable Pie

Total Carbs **11g**
Net Carbs **10g**

prep time:
15 minutes

start to finish:
55 minutes

2 cups chopped broccoli or sliced cauliflowerets

1/3 cup chopped onion

1/3 cup chopped green bell pepper

1 cup shredded reduced-fat Cheddar cheese (4 oz)

1/2 cup Original Bisquick mix

1 cup fat-free (skim) milk

1/2 teaspoon salt

1/4 teaspoon pepper

2 large eggs

1 Heat oven to 400°F. Spray 9-inch glass pie plate with cooking spray. In 2-quart saucepan, heat 1 inch water to boiling. Add broccoli; cover and heat to boiling. Cook about 5 minutes or until almost tender; drain thoroughly.

2 In pie plate, mix broccoli, onion, bell pepper and cheese. In medium bowl, stir remaining ingredients until blended. Pour into pie plate.

3 Bake uncovered 30 to 35 minutes or until golden brown and knife inserted in center comes out clean. Let stand 5 minutes before cutting.

1 serving: Cal. 120 (Cal. from Fat 40); Fat 4.5g (Sat. fat 2g); Chol. 75mg; Sodium 570mg; Net Carbohydrate 10g; Carbs. 11g (Fiber 1g); Pro. 10g | **% daily value:** Vit. A 15%; Vit. C 30%; Calc. 25%; Iron 6% | **exchanges:** 1/2 Starch, 1 Vegetable, 1 Medium-Fat Meat | **CARB. CHOICES:** 1

Impossibly Easy Vegetable Pie

Total Carbs **19g**
Net Carbs **17g**

prep time:
15 minutes

start to finish:
15 minutes

4 wraps

Caesar Salad Wraps

16 small romaine lettuce leaves, torn into bite-size pieces

1/4 cup chopped red onion

2 tablespoons shredded Parmesan or Romano cheese

1/4 cup fat-free Caesar dressing

4 garden vegetable–flavored or plain flour tortillas (6 to 8 inch)

4 hard-cooked large eggs, sliced

2 roma (plum) tomatoes, sliced

1 In large bowl, toss romaine, onion, cheese and dressing to coat.

2 Spread romaine mixture evenly down center of each tortilla. Top with eggs and tomatoes.

3 Fold up one end of tortilla about 1 inch over filling; fold right and left sides over folded end, overlapping. Secure with toothpick if necessary. Serve immediately.

1 wrap: Cal. 190 (Cal. from Fat 70); Fat 8g (Sat. fat 2.5g); Chol. 215mg; Sodium 450mg; Net Carbohydrate 17g; Carbs. 19g (Fiber 2g); Pro. 11g | **% daily value:** Vit. A 30%; Vit. C 30%; Calc. 15%; Iron 10% | **exchanges:** 1 Starch, 1 Vegetable, 1 Medium-Fat Meat, 1/2 Fat | **CARB. CHOICES:** 1

Caesar Salad Wraps

Total Carbs **18g**
Net Carbs **18g**

prep time:
10 minutes

start to finish:
25 minutes

8 servings

Family-Favorite Cheese Pizza

1 1/2 cups Reduced Fat Bisquick mix

1/3 cup very hot water

1/2 cup pizza sauce

1/2 teaspoon Italian seasoning

2 cups shredded part-skim mozzarella cheese (8 oz)

5 slices (3/4 oz each) reduced-fat American cheese

1 Move oven rack to lowest position. Heat oven to 450°F. Spray 12-inch pizza pan with cooking spray.

2 In medium bowl, stir Bisquick mix and very hot water until soft dough forms; beat vigorously with spoon 20 strokes. Press dough in pizza pan, using fingers dipped in Bisquick mix; pinch edge to form 1/2-inch rim.

3 Spread pizza sauce over dough. Sprinkle with Italian seasoning and mozzarella cheese. Bake 10 to 12 minutes or until crust is golden and cheese is bubbly.

4 Cut American cheese into desired shapes with 2-inch cookie cutters. Arrange shapes on pizza. Let stand 1 to 2 minutes or until American cheese is melted.

1 serving: Cal. 200 (Cal. from Fat 80); Fat 9g (Sat. fat 5g); Chol. 20mg; Sodium 650mg; Net Carbohydrate 18g; Carbs. 18g (Fiber 0g); Pro. 12g | **% daily value:** Vit. A 6%; Vit. C 2%; Calc. 30%; Iron 6% | **exchanges:** 1 Starch, 1 1/2 Lean Meat, 1 Fat | **CARB. CHOICES:** 1

Family-Favorite Cheese Pizza

prep time:
15 minutes

start to finish:
15 minutes

4 servings

Vegetable Kung Pao

1/2 cup dry-roasted peanuts

Cooking spray

1 tablespoon cornstarch

1 teaspoon sugar

1 tablespoon cold water

1/2 cup vegetable broth

1 teaspoon chili puree with garlic

1 bag (1 lb) frozen whole carrots, green beans and yellow (wax) beans (or other combination)

Hot cooked brown rice, if desired

1 Heat 12-inch nonstick skillet or nonstick wok over medium-high heat. Spread peanuts in single layer on paper towel; lightly spray with cooking spray, about 2 seconds. Add peanuts to skillet; cook and stir about 1 minute or until toasted. Immediately remove from skillet; cool.

2 In small bowl, mix cornstarch, sugar and cold water; set aside. In skillet, mix broth and chili puree; heat to boiling. Stir in vegetables. Heat to boiling; reduce heat to medium-low. Cover and cook 5 minutes, stirring occasionally.

3 Move vegetables to side of skillet. Stir cornstarch mixture into liquid in skillet. Cook and stir vegetables and sauce over high heat about 1 minute or until sauce is thickened. Stir in peanuts. Serve with rice.

1 serving: Cal. 160 (Cal. from Fat 80); Fat 9g (Sat. fat 1.5g); Chol. 0mg; Sodium 360mg; Net Carbohydrate 11g; Carbs. 16g (Fiber 5g); Pro. 7g | **% daily value:** Vit. A 230%; Vit. C 2%; Calc. 6%; Iron 8% | **exchanges:** 1/2 Starch, 1 Vegetable, 1/2 High-Fat Meat, 1 Fat | **CARB. CHOICES:** 1

4 servings

Savory Vegetable Stew

1 tablespoon olive or vegetable oil

2 cups frozen stir-fry bell peppers and onions (from 1-lb bag)

1 can (14.5 oz) diced tomatoes with mild green chilies, undrained

1 teaspoon chopped fresh or 1/4 teaspoon dried thyme leaves

prep time:
20 minutes

start to finish:
20 minutes

1 In 12-inch nonstick skillet, heat oil over medium-high heat. Cook stir-fry vegetables in oil about 3 minutes, stirring frequently, until crisp-tender.

2 Stir in tomatoes and thyme. Heat to boiling; reduce heat. Cover and simmer 8 to 10 minutes, stirring occasionally, until heated through.

1 serving: Cal. 90 (Cal. from Fat 35); Fat 3.5g (Sat. fat 0g); Chol. 0mg; Sodium 280mg; Net Carbohydrate 11g; Carbs. 13g (Fiber 2g); Pro. 2g | **% daily value:** Vit. A 8%; Vit. C 35%; Calc. 4%; Iron 4% | **exchanges:** 2 Vegetable, 1 Fat | **CARB. CHOICES:** 1

Total Carbs **19g**
Net Carbs **15g**

prep time:
15 minutes

start to finish:
15 minutes

4 servings

Vegetable-Rice Skillet

1 can (14 oz) vegetable broth

1 tablespoon butter or margarine

1 bag (1 lb) frozen broccoli, carrots and cauliflower

1 package (6.2 oz) fast-cooking long-grain and wild rice mix

3/4 cup shredded reduced-fat Cheddar cheese (3 oz)

1 In 10-inch skillet, heat broth and butter to boiling. Stir in vegetables, rice and contents of seasoning packet. Heat to boiling; reduce heat.

2 Cover and simmer 5 to 6 minutes or until vegetables and rice are tender. Sprinkle with cheese.

1 serving: Cal. 150 (Cal. from Fat 40); Fat 4.5g (Sat. fat 2.5g); Chol. 10mg; Sodium 670mg; Net Carbohydrate 15g; Carbs. 19g (Fiber 4g); Pro. 9g | **% daily value:** Vit. A 70%; Vit. C 30%; Calc. 20%; Iron 6% | **exchanges:** 1 Starch, 1 Vegetable, 1/2 High-Fat Meat | **CARB. CHOICES:** 1

Vegetable-Rice Skillet

Total Carbs **18g**
Net Carbs **13g**

prep time:
15 minutes

start to finish:
15 minutes

4 servings

Garden Vegetable Salad

3 cups bite-size pieces cauliflower (1 lb)

2 cups bite-size pieces broccoli (5 oz)

1 cup cherry tomatoes, cut in half

3/4 cup diced reduced-fat Cheddar or Colby cheese

1 medium stalk celery, sliced (1/2 cup)

1/4 cup pimiento-stuffed salad olives

1/2 cup fat-free ranch dressing

1 In large bowl, mix all ingredients except dressing.

2 Add dressing; toss until vegetables are evenly coated.

1 serving: Cal. 130 (Cal. from Fat 40); Fat 4g (Sat. fat 1.5g); Chol. 5mg; Sodium 660mg; Net Carbohydrate 13g; Carbs. 18g (Fiber 5g); Pro. 9g | **% daily value:** Vit. A 25%; Vit. C 140%; Calc. 25%; Iron 8% | **exchanges:** 1/2 Other Carb., 1 1/2 Vegetable, 1 Medium-Fat Meat | **CARB. CHOICES:** 1

4 servings

Cream of Broccoli Soup

Total Carbs **12g**
Net Carbs **8g**

prep time:
30 minutes

start to finish:
30 minutes

1 tablespoon vegetable oil or butter

1 medium onion, chopped (1/2 cup)

2 medium carrots, thinly sliced (1 cup)

2 teaspoons mustard seed

1/2 teaspoon salt

1/4 teaspoon pepper

3/4 lb broccoli, coarsely chopped (3 1/2 cups)

1 can (14 oz) vegetable broth

1 cup water

2 teaspoons lemon juice

1/4 cup light sour cream

1 In 3-quart saucepan, heat oil over medium heat. Cook onion and carrots in oil about 5 minutes, stirring occasionally, until onion is tender. Stir in mustard seed, salt and pepper. Stir in broccoli, broth and water. Heat to boiling; reduce heat. Cover and simmer about 10 minutes or until broccoli is tender.

2 In blender, place one-third of the broccoli mixture. Cover and blend on high speed until smooth; pour into bowl. Continue to blend in small batches until all soup is pureed.

3 Return blended soup to saucepan. Stir in lemon juice. Heat over low heat just until hot. Stir in sour cream.

1 serving: Cal. 110 (Cal. from Fat 50); Fat 6g (Sat. fat 1.5g); Chol. 5mg; Sodium 770mg; Net Carbohydrate 8g; Carbs. 12g (Fiber 4g); Pro. 6g | **% daily value:** Vit. A 130%; Vit. C 60%; Calc. 8%; Iron 8% | **exchanges:** 1/2 Starch, 1 Vegetable, 1 Fat | **CARB. CHOICES:** 1

Chunky Tomato Soup

Total Carbs **12g**
Net Carbs **9g**

prep time:
15 minutes

start to finish:
**1 hour
35 minutes**

2 tablespoons olive or vegetable oil

2 cloves garlic, finely chopped

2 medium stalks celery, coarsely chopped (1 cup)

2 medium carrots, coarsely chopped (1 cup)

2 cans (28 oz each) Italian-style (plum) tomatoes, undrained

2 cups water

1 teaspoon dried basil leaves

1/2 teaspoon pepper

2 cans (14 oz each) vegetable broth

1 In 5- to 6-quart Dutch oven, heat oil over medium-high heat. Cook garlic, celery and carrots in oil 5 to 7 minutes, stirring frequently, until carrots are crisp-tender.

2 Stir in tomatoes, breaking up tomatoes coarsely. Stir in water, basil, pepper and broth. Heat to boiling; reduce heat to low.

3 Cover and simmer 1 hour, stirring occasionally.

1 serving: Cal. 90 (Cal. from Fat 40); Fat 4.5g (Sat. fat 0.5g); Chol. 0mg; Sodium 740mg; Net Carbohydrate 9g; Carbs. 12g (Fiber 3g); Pro. 4g | **% daily value:** Vit. A 70%; Vit. C 25%; Calc. 8%; Iron 8% | **exchanges:** 1/2 Starch, 1 Vegetable, 1 Fat | **CARB. CHOICES:** 1

Chunky Tomato Soup

Zucchini Pancakes

Total Carbs **2g**
Net Carbs **2g**

prep time:
35 minutes

start to finish:
35 minutes

carb-bit

The shredded zucchini, a carb-counter's favorite, adds a great texture to these pancakes. It also offers a delicious way to use up the summertime surplus.

2 large eggs

1/3 cup Original Bisquick mix

1/4 cup grated Parmesan cheese

2 tablespoons chopped onion

Dash of pepper

1 medium zucchini, shredded (2 cups)

Ketchup or sour cream, if desired

1 Heat griddle or skillet over medium heat or to 375°F. Grease griddle with vegetable oil if necessary (or spray with cooking spray before heating).

2 In medium bowl, beat eggs with hand beater until fluffy. Beat in remaining ingredients except zucchini and ketchup until well blended. Fold in zucchini.

3 For each pancake, pour 2 tablespoons batter onto hot griddle; spread slightly with back of spoon. Cook until puffed and dry around edges. Turn; cook until golden brown. Serve with ketchup.

1 pancake: Cal. 25 (Cal. from Fat 10); Fat 1.5g (Sat. fat 0.5g); Chol. 25mg; Sodium 65mg; Net Carbohydrate 2g; Carbs. 2g (Fiber 0g); Pro. 2g | **% daily value:** Vit. A 2%; Vit. C 0%; Calc. 2%; Iron 0% | **exchanges:** 1/2 Fat | **CARB. CHOICES:** 0

7 Side Dish Sampler

Sesame Pea Pods   190

Harvest Roasted Vegetables   192

Asparagus with Maple-Mustard
    Sauce   193

Three-Pepper Stir-Fry   194

Tarragon Tomato Slices   195

Garlic Green Beans   196

Hot and Spicy Greens   198

Bacon-Spinach Salad   199

Greek Salad   200

Sherried Greens with Fruit and Blue
    Cheese   202

Lime-Mint Melon Salad   204

Asian Coleslaw   206

Creamy Dilled Cucumbers   208

◖ = **super express** ready in 30 minutes or less

Total Carbs **4g**
Net Carbs **2g**

prep time:
15 minutes

start to finish:
15 minutes

6 servings

Sesame Pea Pods

I tablespoon sesame oil

8 oz snow (Chinese) pea pods (2 cups)

I tablespoon sesame seed

I medium red or yellow bell pepper, cut into thin strips

1 In 10-inch skillet, heat oil over medium-high heat. Add pea pods and sesame seed. Cook about 2 minutes, stirring frequently, until pea pods are crisp-tender.

2 Stir in bell pepper. Cook about 2 minutes, stirring frequently, until bell pepper is crisp-tender.

I serving: Cal. 45 (Cal. from Fat 30); Fat 3g (Sat. fat 0g); Chol. 0mg; Sodium 0mg; Net Carbohydrate 2g; Carbs. 4g (Fiber 2g); Pro. 2g | **% daily value:** Vit. A 25%; Vit. C 45%; Calc. 0%; Iron 4% | **exchanges:** I Vegetable, 1/2 Fat | **CARB. CHOICES:** 0

Sesame Pea Pods

Total Carbs **7g**
Net Carbs **5g**

prep time:
20 minutes

start to finish:
20 minutes

4 servings

Harvest Roasted Vegetables

**I medium green bell pepper, cut into
I-inch pieces**

**I medium onion, cut into 1/4-inch
wedges**

**I medium tomato, cut into 1/4-inch
wedges**

**I medium zucchini, cut into I-inch
pieces**

Olive oil-flavored cooking spray

1/2 teaspoon salt

1 Set oven control to broil. Cover cookie sheet with foil; spray with cooking spray. Place vegetables in single layer on cookie sheet. Spray vegetables with cooking spray. Sprinkle with 1/4 teaspoon of the salt.

2 Broil with tops 4 inches from heat about 12 minutes, stirring occasionally, until vegetables are tender. Sprinkle with remaining 1/4 teaspoon salt.

I serving: Cal. 30 (Cal. from Fat 0); Fat 0g (Sat. fat 0g); Chol. 0mg; Sodium 300mg; Net Carbohydrate 5g; Carbs. 7g (Fiber 2g); Pro. Ig | **% daily value:** Vit. A 15%; Vit. C 30%; Calc. 0%; Iron 4% | **exchanges:** I Vegetable | **CARB. CHOICES:** 1/2

8 servings

Asparagus with Maple-Mustard Sauce

2 lb asparagus, cut into 2-inch pieces

2 tablespoons real maple syrup or maple-flavored syrup

2 tablespoons Dijon mustard

1 tablespoon olive or vegetable oil

1 In 12-inch skillet or Dutch oven, heat 1 inch water to boiling. Add asparagus. Heat to boiling; reduce heat to medium. Cover and cook 4 to 5 minutes or until asparagus is crisp-tender; drain.

2 In small bowl, mix maple syrup, mustard and oil. Drizzle over asparagus.

 super *express*

Total Carbs **6g**
Net Carbs **6g**

prep time:
15 minutes

start to finish:
15 minutes

1 serving: Cal. 50 (Cal. from Fat 20); Fat 2g (Sat. fat 0g); Chol. 0mg; Sodium 95mg; Net Carbohydrate 6g; Carbs. 6g (Fiber 0g); Pro. 2g | **% daily value:** Vit. A 10%; Vit. C 10%; Calc. 0%; Iron 2% | **exchanges:** 1 Vegetable, 1/2 Fat | **CARB. CHOICES:** 1/2

Total Carbs **8g**
Net Carbs **7g**

prep time:
20 minutes

start to finish:
20 minutes

4 servings

Three-Pepper Stir-Fry

3/4 cup fat-free chicken broth

2 teaspoons grated gingerroot

2 cloves garlic, finely chopped

1 medium red bell pepper, thinly sliced

1 medium yellow bell pepper, thinly sliced

1 medium orange or green bell pepper, thinly sliced

1 tablespoon hoisin sauce

1 In 10-inch nonstick skillet or nonstick wok, heat half of the broth to boiling over medium-high heat. Add gingerroot and garlic; cook and stir 1 minute.

2 Add bell peppers and remaining broth. Cook 5 to 8 minutes, stirring occasionally, until vegetables are tender and most of liquid has evaporated. Stir in hoisin sauce.

1 serving: Cal. 40 (Cal. from Fat 0); Fat 0g (Sat. fat 0g); Chol. 0mg; Sodium 160mg; Net Carbohydrate 7g; Carbs. 8g (Fiber 1g); Pro. 1g | **% daily value:** Vit. A 40%; Vit. C 140%; Calc. 0%; Iron 4% | **exchanges:** 1 Vegetable | **CARB. CHOICES:** 1/2

6 servings

Tarragon Tomato Slices

Total Carbs **4g**
Net Carbs **3g**

prep time:
10 minutes

start to finish:
2 hours
10 minutes

3 medium tomatoes, cut into 1/4-inch slices

1/4 cup tarragon wine vinegar or cider vinegar

1 tablespoon olive or vegetable oil

1 tablespoon chopped fresh or
1 teaspoon dried tarragon leaves

Freshly ground pepper

Lettuce leaves

1 In glass or plastic dish, place tomatoes. In tightly covered container, shake vinegar, oil and tarragon; pour over tomatoes. Sprinkle with pepper.

2 Cover and refrigerate at least 2 hours to blend flavors. Serve on lettuce.

1 serving: Cal. 40 (Cal. from Fat 25); Fat 2.5g (Sat. fat 0g); Chol. 0mg; Sodium 5mg; Net Carbohydrate 3g; Carbs. 4g (Fiber 1g); Pro. 0g | **% daily value:** Vit. A 10%; Vit. C 20%; Calc. 0%; Iron 2% | **exchanges:** 1/2 Vegetable, 1/2 Fat | **CARB. CHOICES:** 0

Total Carbs **5g**
Net Carbs **3g**

prep time:
20 minutes

start to finish:
20 minutes

6 servings

Garlic Green Beans

I lb green beans

I tablespoon butter or margarine

2 teaspoons chopped fresh or
1/2 teaspoon dried oregano leaves

I teaspoon finely chopped garlic

1/4 teaspoon salt

1/4 cup pitted Kalamata olives, cut in half

1 In 2-quart saucepan, add 1 inch of water; add beans. Heat to boiling; reduce heat. Simmer uncovered 6 to 8 minutes or until crisp-tender; drain.

2 In same saucepan, heat butter, oregano, garlic and salt over medium heat 1 to 2 minutes, stirring occasionally. Add beans and olives; toss to coat.

I serving: Cal. 40 (Cal. from Fat 25); Fat 2.5g (Sat. fat 1g); Chol. 5mg; Sodium 170mg; Net Carbohydrate 3g; Carbs. 5g (Fiber 2g); Pro. 1g | **% daily value:** Vit. A 10%; Vit. C 2%; Calc. 4%; Iron 4% | **exchanges:** 1 Vegetable, 1/2 Fat | **CARB. CHOICES:** 0

Garlic Green Beans

super *express*

Total Carbs **7g**
Net Carbs **3g**

prep time:
20 minutes

start to finish:
20 minutes

6 servings

Hot and Spicy Greens

2 tablespoons butter or margarine

2 lb collard greens or spinach, coarsely chopped

I serrano chili, seeded, finely chopped*

2 tablespoons finely chopped onion

I to 2 teaspoons grated gingerroot

1 In 4-quart Dutch oven, melt butter over medium heat.

2 Cook remaining ingredients in butter, stirring frequently, until greens and onion are tender; drain.

*1 jalapeño chili can be substituted for the serrano chili.

I serving: Cal. 70 (Cal. from Fat 40); Fat 4.5g (Sat. fat 2g); Chol. 10mg; Sodium 50mg; Net Carbohydrate 3g; Carbs. 7g (Fiber 4g); Pro. 3g | **% daily value:** Vit. A 130%; Vit. C 50%; Calc. 15%; Iron 0% | **exchanges:** I Vegetable, I Fat | **CARB. CHOICES:** 1/2

4 servings

Bacon-Spinach Salad

4 slices bacon, diced

1/4 cup white vinegar

4 teaspoons sugar

1/4 teaspoon salt

1/8 teaspoon pepper

1 bag (10 oz) washed fresh spinach

5 medium green onions, sliced (1/3 cup)

1 In 12-inch skillet, cook bacon over medium heat, stirring occasionally, until crisp. Stir in vinegar, sugar, salt and pepper. Heat through, stirring constantly, until sugar is dissolved; remove from heat.

2 Add spinach and onions to bacon mixture. Toss 1 to 2 minutes or until spinach is wilted.

Total Carbs **8g**
Net Carbs **5g**

prep time:
15 minutes

start to finish:
15 minutes

For a touch of sweetness and color, use raspberry vinegar instead of white vinegar and artificial sweetener for the sugar. Then, as a final touch, sprinkle the salad with fresh raspberries.

1 serving: Cal. 80 (Cal. from Fat 40); Fat 4g (Sat. fat 1.5g); Chol. 5mg; Sodium 330mg; Net Carbohydrate 5g; Carbs. 8g (Fiber 3g); Pro. 5g | **% daily value:** Vit. A 130%; Vit. C 35%; Calc. 8%; Iron 10% | **exchanges:** 1 1/2 Vegetable, 1 Fat | **CARB. CHOICES:** 1/2

Total Carbs **7g**
Net Carbs **5g**

prep time:
10 minutes

start to finish:
10 minutes

4 servings

Greek Salad

1 medium unpeeled cucumber

2 cups bite-size pieces spinach

2 cups bite-size pieces lettuce

1 medium tomato, cut into thin wedges

1 medium green onion, sliced
(1 tablespoon)

1/3 cup fat-free Caesar dressing

1/4 cup crumbled feta cheese

1 tablespoon sliced ripe olives

1 Score cucumber by running tines of fork lengthwise down sides; cut into slices.

2 In large bowl, toss cucumber and remaining ingredients.

1 serving: Cal. 60 (Cal. from Fat 25); Fat 2.5g (Sat. fat 1.5g); Chol. 10mg; Sodium 420mg; Net Carbohydrate 5g; Carbs. 7g (Fiber 2g); Pro. 3g | **% daily value:** Vit. A 40%; Vit. C 25%; Calc. 10%; Iron 6% | **exchanges:** 1 1/2 Vegetable, 1/2 Fat | **CARB. CHOICES:** 1/2

Greek Salad

Total Carbs **9g**
Net Carbs **7g**

prep time:
15 minutes

start to finish:
15 minutes

8 servings

Sherried Greens with Fruit and Blue Cheese

1/4 cup dry sherry or apple juice

2 tablespoons balsamic or red wine vinegar

1 tablespoon sugar

1 teaspoon toasted sesame oil

8 cups bite-size pieces mixed salad greens

1 medium pear, thinly sliced

1 cup sliced strawberries

1 small red onion, thinly sliced

1/4 cup finely crumbled blue cheese (1 oz)

1 In small bowl, mix sherry, vinegar, sugar and oil until sugar is dissolved.

2 On 8 salad plates, arrange salad greens, pear, strawberries and onion. Pour sherry mixture over salads. Sprinkle with cheese.

1 serving: Cal. 50 (Cal. from Fat 15); Fat 2g (Sat. fat 1g); Chol. 0mg; Sodium 65mg; Net Carbohydrate 7g; Carbs. 9g (Fiber 2g); Pro. 2g | **% daily value:** Vit. A 35%; Vit. C 40%; Calc. 6%; Iron 4% | **exchanges:** 1 Vegetable, 1/2 Fat | **CARB. CHOICES:** 1/2

Sherried Greens with Fruit and Blue Cheese

Lime-Mint Melon Salad

prep time:
10 minutes

start to finish:
**2 hours
10 minutes**

carb-
bit
**Cut carbs by
using a packet or
two of artificial
sweetener (no
calories and less
than 1 gram of
carbs) instead of
honey, which has
21 calories per
teaspoon and
almost 6 grams
of carbs.**

1 1/2 cups 1/2-inch cubes honeydew melon (1/2 medium)

1 1/2 cups 1/2-inch cubes cantaloupe (1/2 medium)

1 teaspoon grated lime peel

3 tablespoons lime juice

2 tablespoons chopped fresh or
1 tablespoon dried mint leaves

1 teaspoon honey

1/4 teaspoon salt

1 In medium glass or plastic bowl, toss all ingredients.

2 Cover and refrigerate about 2 hours or until chilled.

1 serving: Cal. 40 (Cal. from Fat 0); Fat 0g (Sat. fat 0g); Chol. 0mg; Sodium 110mg; Net Carbohydrate 9g; Carbs. 9g (Fiber 0g); Pro. 0g | **% daily value:** Vit. A 25%; Vit. C 50%; Calc. 0%; Iron 0% | **exchanges:** 1/2 Fruit | **CARB. CHOICES:** 1/2

Lime-Mint Melon Salad

Total Carbs **6g**
Net Carbs **5g**

prep time:
15 minutes

start to finish:
15 minutes

4 servings

Asian Coleslaw

Sesame Dressing

3 tablespoons rice vinegar or white wine vinegar

2 teaspoons sugar

2 teaspoons sesame seed, toasted*

2 teaspoons reduced-sodium soy sauce

I teaspoon sesame oil

1/8 teaspoon crushed red pepper flakes

Coleslaw

2 cups finely shredded Chinese (napa) cabbage (8 oz)

1/4 cup chopped jicama

1/4 cup chopped green bell pepper

1/4 cup coarsely shredded carrot

1 In large bowl, mix all dressing ingredients.

2 Add all coleslaw ingredients; toss.

To toast sesame seed, cook in ungreased heavy skillet over medium-low heat 5 to 7 minutes, stirring frequently until browning begins, then stirring constantly until golden brown.

I serving: Cal. 40 (Cal. from Fat 15); Fat 2g (Sat. fat 0g); Chol. 0mg; Sodium 115mg; Net Carbohydrate 5g; Carbs. 6g (Fiber 1g); Pro. 1g | **% daily value:** Vit. A 50%; Vit. C 45%; Calc. 4%; Iron 4% | **exchanges:** I Vegetable, 1/2 Fat | **CARB. CHOICES:** 1/2

Asian Coleslaw

Creamy Dilled Cucumbers

Total Carbs **4g**
Net Carbs **4g**

prep time:
10 minutes

start to finish:
**4 hours
10 minutes**

1/2 cup plain fat-free yogurt

1 teaspoon chopped fresh or
1/4 teaspoon dried dill weed

1/2 teaspoon salt

1/8 teaspoon pepper

2 small cucumbers, sliced (2 cups)

1 small red onion, thinly sliced and
separated into rings

1 In large glass or plastic bowl, mix all ingredients.

2 Cover and refrigerate at least 4 hours to blend flavors.

1 serving: Cal. 20 (Cal. from Fat 0); Fat 0g (Sat. fat 0g); Chol. 0mg; Sodium 210mg; Net Carbohydrate 4g; Carbs. 4g (Fiber 0g); Pro. 2g | **% daily value:** Vit. A 0%; Vit. C 4%; Calc. 4%; Iron 0% | **exchanges:** 1 Vegetable | **CARB. CHOICES:** 0

Creamy Dilled Cucumbers

Carb-Smart Snacks and Desserts

Snacks can be an important part of a weight-loss plan because they may help hold off hunger so you don't overindulge at the next meal. And almost everyone looks forward to a little something sweet for dessert now and again! It's all about options, so satisfy your cravings with the many choices below, all with approximately 9 carbs or less and 3 grams of fat or less.

Just a Little Snack

Food	How Much	Extras	Calories
Bell pepper slices	1/2 cup	1 Tbsp fat-free salad dressing	12 without extras 30 with extras
Broccoli or cauliflower flowerets	1/2 cup	1 Tbsp fat-free salad dressing	12 without extras 30 with extras
Carrots, baby	8	1 Tbsp fat-free salad dressing	22 without extras 40 with extras
Cucumber slices	1/2 cup	1 Tbsp fat-free salad dressing	7 without extras 25 with extras
Melon wedge	5x1 inch	Lime wedges	24 with or without extras
Grape tomatoes	5	1 Tbsp fat-free salad dressing	18 without extras 36 with extras
Hummus	1 Tbsp	1/2 cup cucumber slices or bell pepper strips	About 42
Reduced-fat peanut butter spread on 2-inch piece of celery	2 tsp peanut butter		70
Fat-free cottage cheese	1/2 cup		74
Fresh mozzarella cheese balls	4 (1 inch)		213
Mozzarella string cheese (part-skim)	1 string		63
Reduced-fat microwave popcorn	1 cup	1 tsp reduced-fat Parmesan cheese	27 without extras 35 with extras
Rice cakes, mini	4 (2 inch)		64
Thin pretzel sticks	20 (2 1/4 inch)		46

For Dessert!

Food	How Much	Extras	Calories
Apricot	1 small		17
Bing cherries	6		29
Berries	1/2 cup	1 Tbsp fat-free frozen whipped topping or fat-free half-and-half	22 without extras 28 with topping 31 with half-and-half
Grapes	10	Dip in 1 Tbsp reduced-fat sour cream or freeze grapes for an icy version	43 without extras 63 with extras
Fruit-flavored pops, sugar-free	1	13	
Fudge pops, fat-free	1		26
Fruit-flavored gelatin, sugar-free	1/2 cup	1 Tbsp fat-free frozen whipped topping	8 without extras 14 with extras

"Carb-Wise" Carbohydrate, Fat and Calorie Count of Common Foods

Here is your at-a-glance look at some common foods and the number of total carbohydrates, fat and calories they have:

Food	How Much	Carbohydrate Grams	Fat	Calories
Grains / Beans / Starchy Vegetables				
Bagel	1 large			
White		38	1	95
Whole wheat		45	0.5	210
Baked beans	1/2 cup	25	1.5	124
Beans (pinto, garbanzo, kidney), cooked	1/2 cup	22	0.5	117
Bread	1 slice (1 oz)			
White		14	2	84
Whole wheat		13	1	69
Cereal, whole-grain unsweetened	3/4 cup	17	1.5	83
Dinner roll	1 small (1 oz)			
White		14	2	84
Whole wheat		13	1	69
English muffin	2 oz			
White		23	1	133
Whole wheat		29	1	115
Hamburger or hot dog bun	2 oz			
White		29	3	162
Whole wheat		26	2.5	139
Pancakes	2 (4 inch)	27	2	145
Pasta, white (macaroni, noodles, spaghetti), cooked	1 cup	40	1	197
Rice, cooked	1/2 cup			
White		22	0	103
Brown		22	1	108
Wild		18	0.5	83
Corn, cooked	1/2 cup	16	0.5	66
Peas, green, cooked	1/2 cup	11	0	62
Potato, white, baked or boiled	1 medium	21	0	91
Potato, white or red, mashed	1/2 cup	18	5.5	128
Potato, sweet, baked or boiled	1 medium	28	0	117
Winter squash, cooked	1/2 cup	11	1	47
Tortilla, flour	1 (6 inch)			
White		13	1.5	78
Whole wheat		9	0.5	47
Waffle	1 (4 1/2 inch)	16	4	112

continues on next page

Food	How Much	Carbohydrate Grams	Fat	Calories
Fruits / Fruit Juices				
Apple, orange or pear	1 medium	21	0.5	81
Banana	1 medium	28	0.5	109
Berries	1 cup			
(blueberries,		20	0.5	81
raspberries or		14	0.5	60
strawberries)		10	0.5	43
Cherries	12 to 15	17	1	73
Grapes	12 to 15	13	0.5	53
Grapefruit	1/2 medium	10	0	38
Kiwifruit	1	11	0.5	46
Mango	1/2 cup	14	0	54
Melon	1 cup	11	0.5	49
Nectarine	1 medium	16	0.5	67
Orange	1 medium	15	0	62
Orange juice	1/2 cup	14	0	56
Peach	1 medium	11	0	42
Pineapple	1/2 cup	10	0.5	38
Plums				
Dried	3	16	0	60
Fresh	1 small	7	0.5	30
Raisins	2 tablespoons	14	0	54

Food	How Much	Carbohydrate Grams	Fat	Calories
Liquid Dairy Products/Yogurt/Liquid Dairy Substitutes				
Fat-free (skim) milk	1 cup	12	0	86
1% milk	1 cup	12	3	102
2% milk	1 cup	11	5	122
Whole milk	1 cup	11	8	149
Whipping (heavy) cream	1 cup	7	88	821
Half-and-half	1 cup	10	28	315
Fat-free half-and-half	1 cup	22	3.5	143
Soy milk	1 cup			
Low-fat		9	3	90
Fat-free		16	1	82
Yogurt, strawberry, low-fat, artificially sweetened	1 cup	47	3	250
Yogurt, strawberry, low-fat, sweetened with fruit	1 cup	47	3	250

Food	How Much	Carbohydrate Grams	Fat	Calories
Snacks / Sweets				
Brownie or cake, frosted	2-inch square	32	15	263
Chips, potato or tortilla	10 to 15 chips	17	6.5	136
Chocolate snack-size candy bar	1 oz	17	8.5	145
Crackers, graham	3 squares	16	2	83
Crackers, saltines	6 squares	13	2.5	80
Crackers, snack	4 or 5 crackers			
White		9	4.5	81
Whole-grain		14	3.0	91
Doughnut, glazed	1 (3 inch)	20	9	170
Frozen yogurt, vanilla	1/2 cup			
Low-fat		29	2	149
Fat-free		23	0	108
Frozen sugar-free yogurt, vanilla	1/2 cup			
Low-fat		18	2	103
Fat-free		18	0	83
Gelatin, flavored	1/2 cup			
Regular		39	0	162
Sugar-free		1	0	8
Hard candies	3 round			
Regular		18	0	71
Sugar-free		9	0	23
Ice cream, premium, vanilla	1/2 cup			
Light		17	5	124
Sugar-free		12	4	99
Sugar-free light		14	5	112
Jam or jelly, strawberry	1 Tbsp			
Regular		14	0	56
Low-sugar		9	0	36
Sugar-free		3	0	11
Muffin, blueberry	1 large	33	7	207
Pudding, chocolate	1/2 cup			
Regular		28	3	149
Sugar-free		13	3	90
Sugar	1 Tbsp			
Brown		13	0	52
Granulated		13	0	48
Honey	1 Tbsp	17	0	64
Maple-flavored syrup	1 Tbsp	15	0	55
NutraSweet® sweetener	1 Tbsp	9	0	37
SPLENDA® no calorie sweetener	1 Tbsp	0	0	0

continues on next page

Food	How Much	Carbohydrate Grams	Fat	Calories
Vegetables (nonstarchy)				
Asparagus, cooked	1/2 cup pieces	4	0.5	25
	8 spears	4	0.5	25
Beans, green, cooked	1/2 cup	4	0	19
Beets, cooked	1/2 cup	8	0	37
Broccoli flowerets	1 cup raw	5	0.5	25
	1/2 cup cooked	5	0	26
Cabbage, green, shredded	1/2 cup raw	4	0	18
	1/2 cup cooked	3	0.5	17
Carrots, baby-cut	1/2 cup raw	8	0	33
	1/2 cup cooked	8	0	35
Cauliflower flowerets	1 cup raw	5	0	25
	1/2 cup cooked	3	0	17
Celery, raw	1 medium stalk	1	0	6
Cucumber, raw	1/2 cup	1	0	7
Eggplant, cooked	1/2 cup	3	0	14
Lettuce, iceberg or romaine	1 cup	1	0	7
Mushrooms	1 cup raw whole	4	0.5	24
	1/2 cup sliced, cooked	4	0.5	21
Pea pods	1 cup raw	4	0	25
	1/2 cup cooked	6	0	34
Spinach	1 cup raw	1	0	7
	1/2 cup cooked	5	0	27
Tomato	1 small (2 1/2 inch)	4	0.5	19
Zucchini	1 cup raw	3	0	16
	1/2 cup cooked	4	0	14

Food	How Much	Carbohydrate Grams	Fat	Calories
Combination Foods				
Burrito, bean, flour tortilla	7 inches long	44	7.5	281
Burrito, ground beef, flour tortilla	7 inches long	29	8.5	243
Chili with ground beef	1 cup	26	8.5	250
Hamburger with bun	3 inches in diameter	29	16	360
Lasagna with ground beef	4x3-inch piece	32	18	407
Macaroni and cheese	1 cup	48	18	400
Pasta or potato salad	1/2 cup	16	11.5	170

Food	How Much	Carbohydrate Grams	Fat	Calories
Combination Foods (continued)				
Pizza, thick crust (cheese)	1/8 of pizza (from 12-inch pizza)	12	7.5	142
Pizza, thin crust (cheese)	1/8 of pizza (from 12-inch pizza)	8	4	90
Soup	1 cup			
Beef barley		14	1.5	96
Beer cheese		16	11.5	227
Chicken noodle		9	2.5	76
Chicken wild rice		9	2.5	77
Split pea		26	3.5	181
Tomato		18	2.0	92
Spaghetti or pasta sauce (red), purchased	1/2 cup	23	4	127
Alfredo sauce, purchased	1/2 cup	8	38	408
Sub sandwich with ham, turkey and salami or beef and cheese	6 inches long	43	11.5	364
Taco, hard shell, ground beef filling	1	10.5	7.5	138

Recipe Browser—View Total Carb Counts at-a-Glance!

Here it is, an easy, at-a-glance chart showing total carbs per serving for all the recipes in this book. Organized by meal occasion categories, this handy list will let you mix-and-match recipes to fit your personal reduced-carb eating plan.

Recipe Category and Recipe Name	Total Carbs Per Serving
Appetizers and Snacks	
Chicken-Ham Bites	0
Fresh Basil-Wrapped Cheese Balls	0
Gingered Shrimp	0
Gorgonzola- and Hazelnut-Stuffed Mushrooms	0
Spicy Meatballs	0
Thai-Spiced Cocktail Shrimp	0
Easy Salmon Pâté	1
Sautéed Olives	1
Avocado-Seafood Appetizer Bites	2
Bell Pepper Nachos	2
Shrimp Nacho Bites	2
Surf and Turf Kabobs	2
Blue Cheese and Pear Triangles	3
Nacho Cheese Pinwheels	3
Parmesan Puffs with Marinara	3
Bacon-Turkey Bites	4
Chipotle–Black Bean Dip	4
Corn and Olive Spread	4
Greek Appetizer Tarts	4
Layered Vegetable and Aioli Appetizer	4
Zippy Chicken Drummies	4
Asiago Cheese and Artichoke Dip	5
Red Pepper Bruschetta	5
Maple-Glazed Chicken Kabobs	6
Hummus	8
Pineapple-Lime Fruit Dip	8
Chicken Satay	9
Sun-Dried Tomato and Bacon Bruschetta	9
Spinach Quesadillas with Feta Cheese	10
Spiced Pork Tenderloin Crostini	11
Breakfast	
Savory Italian Frittata	2
Pizza Frittata	6
Spring Vegetable Frittata	6

Recipe Category and Recipe Name	Total Carbs Per Serving
Impossibly Easy Ham and Swiss Pie	11
Asian Omelet	15
Spicy Sausage Breakfast Squares	15
Green Chile, Egg and Potato Bake	18
Honey Ham Bagel Sandwiches	18
Potato-Basil Scramble	18
Brunch Eggs on English Muffins	19
Cheesy Ham and Asparagus Bake	19
Vegetable Poached Eggs	19
Whole Wheat Waffles	19
Lunch or Dinner	
Meat	
Italian Roasted Pork Tenderloin	0
Mustard Lamb Chops	0
Sirloin with Bacon-Dijon Sauce	0
Southwestern Pork Chops	0
Broiled Herb Steak	1
Garlicky Pork with Basil	1
Steakhouse Sirloin au Jus	2
Three-Pepper Beef Tenderloin	2
Giant Oven Burger	5
Veal with Asparagus	5
Beef with Spiced Pepper Sauce	6
Meat Loaf	6
Savory Beef Tenderloin	7
Breaded Pork Chops	9
Italian Steak and Vegetables	9
Lamb with Creamy Mint Sauce	10
Pork with Rich Vegetable Gravy	10
Swiss Steak	10
Gingered Flank Steak	11
Spicy Pepper Steak	11
Caramelized Pork Slices	12
Beef Stew, Bologna Style	13
Hearty Beef and Vegetables	13

Recipe Category and Recipe Name	Total Carbs Per Serving
Broiled Dijon Burgers	14
Greek Honey and Lemon Pork Chops	14
Caribbean Pork Tenderloin	15
Honey-Mustard Pork Chops	19
Pork Medallions with Hot Pineapple Glaze	19

Lunch or Dinner

Poultry

Basil and Prosciutto Chicken	0
Hot Seared Chicken	0
Balsamic Chicken	1
Lemon Thyme Chicken Breasts	1
Sesame Ginger Chicken	2
Chicken with Savory Sauce	4
Baked Oregano Chicken	7
Crunchy Herbed Baked Chicken Breasts	7
Chicken in Olive-Wine Sauce	8
Chicken Marsala	8
Italian Chicken Packets	8
Italian Chicken Salad	8
Southwestern Chicken BLT Salad	8
Caribbean Chicken Kabobs	9
Crunchy Garlic Chicken	9
Turkey Tenderloins and Mixed Sweet Peppers	9
Grilled Citrus Chicken	10
Honey-Mustard Turkey with Snap Peas	10
Thai Chicken with Cucumber–Red Onion Relish	10
Wild Mushroom Herbed Chicken	10
Moroccan Chicken	11
Oven-Fried Chicken Nuggets	12
Chicken and Strawberry-Spinach Salad	14
Fiesta Chicken and Rice	14
Easy Salsa Chicken	15
Summer Garden Chicken Stir-Fry	15
Teriyaki Chicken Kabobs	15
California-Style Turkey Patties with Corn and Tomato Relish	16

Lunch or Dinner

Fish and Seafood

Lemon-Garlic Halibut Steaks	2
Savory Shrimp and Scallops	2
Whitefish and Shrimp Cakes	2
Marinated Tuna Steaks with Cucumber Sauce	3

Recipe Category and Recipe Name	Total Carbs Per Serving
Parmesan Perch	3
Gremolata-Topped Sea Bass	6
Broiled Salmon with Orange-Mustard Glaze	7
Grilled Creole Snapper	7
Orange and Dill Pan-Seared Tuna	7
Spinach-Shrimp Salad with Hot Bacon Dressing	7
Southwestern Stir-Fried Shrimp	8
Red Snapper with Mango Salsa	11
Grilled Fish Tacos	13
Grilled Shrimp Kabobs	15
Cornmeal-Crusted Catfish	16

Lunch or Dinner

Vegetarian

Zucchini Pancakes	2
Easy Spinach Pie	9
Eggplant and Gouda Cheese Pie	11
Impossibly Easy Vegetable Pie	11
Cream of Broccoli Soup	12
Chunky Tomato Soup	12
Savory Vegetable Stew	13
Vegetable Kung Pao	16
Eggplant Parmesan	18
Family-Favorite Cheese Pizza	18
Garden Vegetable Salad	18
Caesar Salad Wraps	19
Vegetable-Rice Skillet	19

Sides

Creamy Dilled Cucumbers	4
Sesame Pea Pods	4
Tarragon Tomato Slices	4
Garlic Green Beans	5
Asian Coleslaw	6
Asparagus with Maple-Mustard Sauce	6
Greek Salad	7
Harvest Roasted Vegetables	7
Hot and Spicy Greens	7
Bacon-Spinach Salad	8
Three-Pepper Stir-Fry	8
Lime-Mint Melon Salad	9
Sherried Greens with Fruit and Blue Cheese	9

Helpful Nutrition and Cooking Information

Nutrition Guidelines

We provide nutrition information for each recipe that includes calories, fat, cholesterol, sodium, carbohydrate, fiber and protein. Individual food choices can be based on this information.

Recommended intake for a daily diet of 2,000 calories as set by the Food and Drug Administration

Total Fat	**Less than 65g**
Saturated Fat	**Less than 20g**
Cholesterol	**Less than 300mg**
Sodium	**Less than 2,400mg**
Total Carbohydrate	**300g**
Dietary Fiber	**25g**

Criteria Used for Calculating Nutrition Information

- The first ingredient was used wherever a choice is given (such as 1/3 cup sour cream or plain yogurt).
- The first ingredient amount was used wherever a range is given (such as 3- to 3 1/2-pound cut-up broiler-fryer chicken).
- The first serving number was used wherever a range is given (such as 4 to 6 servings).
- "If desired" ingredients and recipe variations were not included (such as sprinkle with brown sugar, if desired).
- Only the amount of a marinade or frying oil that is estimated to be absorbed by the food during preparation or cooking was calculated.

Ingredients Used in Recipe Testing and Nutrition Calculations

- Ingredients used for testing represent those that the majority of consumers use in their homes: large eggs, 2% milk, 80%-lean ground beef, canned ready-to-use chicken broth and vegetable oil spread containing not less than 65 percent fat.
- Fat-free, low-fat or low-sodium products were not used, unless otherwise indicated.
- Solid vegetable shortening (not butter, margarine, nonstick cooking sprays or vegetable oil spread as they can cause sticking problems) was used to grease pans, unless otherwise indicated.

Equipment Used in Recipe Testing

We use equipment for testing that the majority of consumers use in their homes. If a specific piece of equipment (such as a wire whisk) is necessary for recipe success, it is listed in the recipe.

- Cookware and bakeware without nonstick coatings were used, unless otherwise indicated.
- No dark-colored, black or insulated bakeware was used.
- When a pan is specified in a recipe, a metal pan was used; a baking dish or pie plate means ovenproof glass was used.
- An electric hand mixer was used for mixing only when mixer speeds are specified in the recipe directions. When a mixer speed is not given, a spoon or fork was used.

Cooking Terms Glossary

Beat: Mix ingredients vigorously with spoon, fork, wire whisk, hand beater or electric mixer until smooth and uniform.

Boil: Heat liquid until bubbles rise continuously and break on the surface and steam is given off. For rolling boil, the bubbles form rapidly.

Chop: Cut into coarse or fine irregular pieces with a knife, food chopper, blender or food processor.

Cube: Cut into squares 1/2 inch or larger.

Dice: Cut into squares smaller than 1/2 inch.

Grate: Cut into tiny particles using small rough holes of grater (citrus peel or chocolate).

Grease: Rub the inside surface of a pan with shortening, using pastry brush, piece of waxed paper or paper towel, to prevent food from sticking during baking (as for some casseroles).

Julienne: Cut into thin, matchlike strips, using knife or food processor (vegetables, fruits, meats).

Mix: Combine ingredients in any way that distributes them evenly.

Sauté: Cook foods in hot oil or margarine over medium-high heat with frequent tossing and turning motion.

Shred: Cut into long thin pieces by rubbing food across the holes of a shredder, as for cheese, or by using a knife to slice very thinly, as for cabbage.

Simmer: Cook in liquid just below the boiling point on top of the stove; usually after reducing heat from a boil. Bubbles will rise slowly and break just below the surface.

Stir: Mix ingredients until uniform consistency. Stir once in a while for stirring occasionally, often for stirring frequently and continuously for stirring constantly.

Toss: Tumble ingredients (such as green salad) lightly with a lifting motion, usually to coat evenly or mix with another food.

metric conversion chart

Volume

U.S. Units	Canadian Metric	Australian Metric
1/4 teaspoon	1 mL	1 ml
1/2 teaspoon	2 mL	2 ml
1 teaspoon	5 mL	5 ml
1 tablespoon	15 mL	20 ml
1/4 cup	50 mL	60 ml
1/3 cup	75 mL	80 ml
1/2 cup	125 mL	125 ml
2/3 cup	150 mL	170 ml
3/4 cup	175 mL	190 ml
1 cup	250 mL	250 ml
1 quart	1 liter	1 liter
1 1/2 quarts	1.5 liters	1.5 liters
2 quarts	2 liters	2 liters
2 1/2 quarts	2.5 liters	2.5 liters
3 quarts	3 liters	3 liters
4 quarts	4 liters	4 liters

Weight

U.S. Units	Canadian Metric	Australian Metric
1 ounce	30 grams	30 grams
2 ounces	55 grams	60 grams
3 ounces	85 grams	90 grams
4 ounces (1/4 pound)	115 grams	125 grams
8 ounces (1/2 pound)	225 grams	225 grams
16 ounces (1 pound)	455 grams	500 grams
1 pound	455 grams	1/2 kilogram

Measurements

Inches	Centimeters
1	2.5
2	5.0
3	7.5
4	10.0
5	12.5
6	15.0
7	17.5
8	20.5
9	23.0
10	25.5
11	28.0
12	30.5
13	33.0

Temperatures

Fahrenheit	Celsius
32°	0°
212°	100°
250°	120°
275°	140°
300°	150°
325°	160°
350°	180°
375°	190°
400°	200°
425°	220°
450°	230°
475°	240°
500°	260°

Note: The recipes in this cookbook have not been developed or tested using metric measures. When converting recipes to metric, some variations in quality may be noted.

Index

Page numbers in *italic* indicate illustrations

A

Artichoke, and Asiago Cheese Dip, 47
Asiago Cheese and Artichoke Dip, 47
Asian Coleslaw, 206–207
Asian Omelet, 54
Asparagus
    and Ham Bake, 62
    Italian Steak and Vegetables, 74–75
    with Maple-Mustard Sauce, 193
    Veal with, 90–91
Avocado
    -Seafood Appetizer Bites, 14
    Shrimp Nacho Bites, 34

B

Bacon
    -Dijon Sauce, 78
    Dressing, Hot, 168
    Southwestern Chicken BLT Salad, 142
    -Spinach Salad, 199
    Sun-Dried Tomato Bruschetta and, 43
    -Turkey Bites, 28
Bagels, Honey Ham Sandwich on, 66–67
Baked Oregano Chicken, 137
Balsamic Chicken, 131
Barbecue Sauce, 70
Basil
    -Potato Scramble, 52
    and Prosciutto Chicken, 122–123
    -Wrapped Cheese Balls, 16–17
Bean dip
    Chipotle-Black Bean Dip, 48
    Nacho Cheese Pinwheels, 18–19
Beef
    Burger, Giant Oven, 86
    Burger, Dijon, Broiled, 84–85
    Gingered Flank Steak, 72
    Herb Steak, Broiled, 73
    Italian Steak and Vegetables, 74–75
    Meatballs, Spicy, 30
    Meat Loaf, 87
    Pepper Steak, Spicy, 80
    Sirloin au Jus, Steakhouse, 76
    Sirloin with Bacon-Dijon Sauce, 78
    with Spiced Pepper Sauce, 77
    Stew, Bologna Style, 88–89
    Surf and Turf Kabobs, 31
    Swiss Steak, 79
    Tenderloin, Savory, 82
    Three-Pepper Tenderloin, 83
    Vegetables and, Hearty, 81
Bell Pepper Nachos, 38
Bisquick mix
    Cheese Pizza, Family-Favorite, 178–179
    Ham and Swiss Pie, Impossibly Easy, 60–61
    Vegetable Pie, Impossibly Easy, 174–175
    Zucchini Pancakes, 188
Blue cheese
    Dipping Sauce, 29
    and Pear Triangles, 46
    Sherried Greens with Fruit and, 202–203
Breaded Pork Chops, 92–93

Broccoli
    Garden Vegetable Salad, 184
    Soup, Cream of, 185
    Vegetable Pie, Impossibly Easy, 174–175
    Vegetable Poached Eggs, 53
    Vegetable-Rice Skillet, 182–183
Broiled Dijon Burgers, 84–85
Broiled Herb Steak, 73
Broiled Salmon with Orange-Mustard Glaze, 152
Brunch Eggs on English Muffins, 50–51
Bruschetta
    Red Pepper, 44
    Sun-Dried Tomato and Bacon, 43
Burgers. *See* Beef

C

Cabbage, Chinese, Asian Coleslaw, 206–207
Caesar Salad Wraps, 176–177
California-Style Turkey Patties with Corn and Tomato Relish, 144–145
Cantaloupe, Lime-Mint Melon Salad, 204–205
Caramelized Pork Slices, 101
Caribbean Chicken Kabobs, 116–117
Caribbean Pork Tenderloin, 102–103
Catfish, Cornmeal-Crusted, 157
Cauliflower
    Garden Vegetable Salad, 184
    Vegetable-Rice Skillet, 182–183
Cheddar cheese
    Chipotle-Black Bean Dip, 48
    Garden Vegetable Salad, 184
    Green Chile, Egg and Potato Bake, 63
    Ham and Asparagus Bake, Cheesy, 62
    Herbed Cheese Sauce, 50
    Vegetable Pie, Impossibly Easy, 174–175
    Vegetable-Rice Skillet, 182–183
Cheese
    Basil-Wrapped Cheese Balls, 16–17
    Nacho Cheese Pinwheels, 18–19
    See also specific cheeses
Cheesy Ham and Asparagus Bake, 62
Chicken
    Balsamic, 131
    Basil and Prosciutto, 122–123
    Citrus, Grilled, 114–115
    Drummies, Zippy, 29
    Garlic, Crunchy, 138
    -Ham Bites, 26–27
    Herbed Baked Breasts, Crunchy, 136
    Hot Seared, 119
    Italian Packets, 108–109
    Italian Salad, 120–121
    Kabobs, Caribbean, 116–117
    Lemon Thyme Breasts, 112–113
    Maple-Glazed Kabobs, 24
    Marsala, 128–129
    Moroccan, 126
    Nuggets, Oven-Fried, 139
    in Olive-Wine Sauce, 127
    Oregano, Baked, 137
    and Rice, Fiesta, 141

    Salsa, Easy, 124
    Satay, 25
    Savory Sauce and, 134–135
    Sesame Ginger, 110–111
    Southwestern BLT Salad, 142
    and Strawberry-Spinach Salad, 132–133
    Summer Garden Stir-Fry, 130
    Teriyaki Kabobs, 118
    Thai, with Cucumber-Red Onion Relish, 140
    Wild Mushroom Herbed, 125
Chipotle-Black Bean Dip, 48
Chunky Tomato Soup, 186–187
Citrus Marinade, 71
Colby-Monterey Jack cheese
    Chipotle-Black Bean Dip, 48
    Shrimp Nacho Bites, 34
Collard greens, Hot and Spicy Greens, 198
Cornmeal-Crusted Catfish, 157
Corn and Olive Spread, 21
Corn and Tomato Relish, 144
Crabmeat, imitation, Avocado-Seafood Appetizer Bites, 14
Cranberry sauce, Honey Mustard Sauce and, 28
Creamy Dilled Cucumbers, 208–209
Creamy Mint Sauce, 106
Crostini, Pork Tenderloin, Spicy, 32
Crunchy Garlic Chicken, 138
Crunchy Herbed Baked Chicken Breasts, 136
Cucumbers
    Dilled, Creamy, 208–209
    -Red Onion Relish, 140
    Sauce, 154

D

Dairy products
    common, carb/fat/calorie count, 214
    daily servings, 8
Desserts, low-carb, 212
Diet
    balanced, guidelines for, 7–8
    FDA recommended intake, 218
    low-carb. *See* Low-carb diet
    nutrition calculations in, 218
    portion size, 9
Dipping sauces
    Blue Cheese, 29
    Honey Mustard-Cranberry, 28
Dips and spreads
    Asiago Cheese and Artichoke, 47
    Chipotle-Black Bean, 48
    Corn and Olive, 21
    Hummus, 22
    Pineapple-Lime Fruit Dip, 23
    Salmon Pâté, Easy, 15
Dressings, Hot Bacon, 168

E

Easy Salmon Pâté, 15
Easy Salsa Chicken, 124
Easy Spinach Pie, 173
Eggplant and Gouda Cheese Pie, 172

Eggplant Parmesan, 170–171
Egg product, fat/cholesterol free
    Cheesy Ham and Asparagus Bake, 62
    Eggs on English Muffins, Brunch, 50–51
    Green Chile, Egg and Potato Bake, 63
    Italian Frittata, Savory, 55
    Pizza Frittata, 58–59
    Potato-Basil Scramble, 52
    Spring Vegetable Frittata, 56–57
    Whole Wheat Waffles, 68
Eggs
    Asian Omelet, 54
    Ham and Swiss Pie, Impossibly Easy,
      60–61
    Sausage Breakfast Squares, Spicy, 64–65
    Spinach Pie, Easy, 173
    Vegetable Poached, 53
English muffins, Eggs on, Brunch, 50–51

F

Family-Favorite Cheese Pizza, 178–179
Feta cheese
    Greek Appetizer Tarts, 20
    Spinach Quesadillas with, 42
Fiesta Chicken and Rice, 141
Filberts, Gorgonzola-and-Hazelnut-Stuffed
    Mushrooms, 35
Filo shells, Greek Appetizer Tarts, 20
Fish and seafood
    Grilled Fish Tacos, 158–159
    See also specific types of fish
Fontina cheese, Sun-Dried Tomato and
    Bacon Bruschetta, 43
Fresh Basil-Wrapped Cheese Balls, 16–17
Frittata. *See* Eggs
Fruit
    Caribbean Pork Tenderloin, 102–103
    common, carb/fat/calorie count, 214
    daily servings, 8
    Sherried Greens with Blue Cheese and,
      202–203
    See also specific types of fruit

G

Garbanzo beans, Hummus, 22
Garden Vegetable Salad, 184
Garlic Green Beans, 196–197
Garlic Marinade, 71
Giant Oven Burger, 86
Gingered Flank Steak, 72
Gingered Shrimp, 12–13
Glaze
    Orange-Mustard, 152
    Pineapple, Hot, 98
Gorgonzola cheese
    Basil-Wrapped Cheese Balls, 16–17
    Hazelnut-Stuffed Mushrooms and, 35
Gouda cheese, and Eggplant Cheese Pie, 172
Greek
    Appetizer Tarts, 20
    Honey and Lemon Pork Chops, 97
    Salad, 200–201
Green beans
    Beef and Vegetables, Hearty, 81
    Garlic, 196–197
Green Chile, Egg and Potato Bake, 63
Gremolata-Topped Sea Bass, 148–149
Grilled Citrus Chicken, 114–115
Grilled Creole Snapper, 156
Grilled Fish Tacos, 158–159
Grilled Shrimp Kabobs, 161

H

Halibut, Lemon-Garlic Steaks, 150–151
Ham
    and Asparagus Bake, 62
    -Chicken Bites, 26–27
    Honey Bagel Sandwiches, 66–67
    and Swiss Pie, Impossibly Easy, 60–61
Harvest Roasted Vegetables, 192
Hearty Beef and Vegetables, 81
Herbed Cheese Sauce, 50
Herb Rub, 71
Honeydew, Lime-Mint Melon Salad, 204–205
Honey mustard
    -Cranberry Sauce, 28
    Ham Bagel Sandwiches, 66–67
    Pork Chops, 96
    Turkey with Snap Peas, 146
Hot Bacon Dressing, 168
Hot Pineapple Glaze, 100
Hot Seared Chicken, 119
Hot and Spicy Greens, 198
Hummus, 22

I

Impossibly Easy Ham and Swiss Pie, 60–61
Impossibly Easy Vegetable Pie, 174–175
Italian
    Chicken Packets, 108–109
    Chicken Salad, 120
    Roasted Pork Tenderloin, 104
    Steak and Vegetables, 74–75

K

Kabobs
    Chicken, Maple-Glazed, 24
    Chicken, Caribbean, 116–117
    Chicken Satay, 25
    Chicken, Teriyaki, 118
    Shrimp, Grilled, 161
    Surf and Turf, 31

L

Lamb
    Chops, Mustard, 105
    with Creamy Mint Sauce, 106
Layered Vegetable and Aioli Appetizer,
    40–41
Lemon-Garlic Halibut Steaks, 150–151
Lemon Thyme Chicken Breasts, 112–113
Lime-Mint Melon Salad, 204–205
Low-carb diet
    carb-swaps, 10
    common foods, carb/fat/calories (chart),
      213–217
    and glycemic index, 10
    recipes, carb values of, 210–211
    snacks/desserts, 212

M

Mango Salsa, 155
Maple-Glazed Chicken Kabobs, 24
Maple-Mustard Sauce, 193
Marinades
    Barbecue Sauce, 70
    Citrus, 71
    Garlic, 71
    Mustard, 71
    See also Rubs
Marinara sauce, Parmesan Puffs with, 39

Marinated Tuna Steaks with Cucumber
    Sauce, 154
Meat
    calories/fat per cut, 8
    See also specific types of meat
Meat Loaf, 87
Metric conversion chart, 220
Mexican cheese blend, Spicy Sausage
    Breakfast Squares, 64–65
Mexican Rub, 71
Mint Sauce, Creamy, 106
Monterey Jack cheese, Bell Pepper Nachos, 38
Moroccan Chicken, 126
Mozzarella cheese
    Cheese Pizza, Family-Favorite, 178–179
    Eggplant Parmesan, 170–171
    Vegetable Poached Eggs, 53
Mushrooms
    Beef Tenderloin, Savory, 82
    Chicken-Ham Bites, 26–27
    Chicken Marsala, 128–129
    Chicken with Savory Sauce, 134–135
    Gorgonzola-and-Hazelnut-Stuffed, 35
    Pizza Frittata, 58–59
    Spinach-Shrimp Salad with Hot Bacon
      Dressing, 168
    Veal with Asparagus, 90–91
    Vegetable Poached Eggs, 53
    Wild, Herbed Chicken, 125
Mustard Lamb Chops, 105
Mustard Marinade, 71

N

Nacho Cheese Pinwheels, 18–19

O

Olives
    Chicken in Olive-Wine Sauce, 127
    Corn and, Spread, 21
    Sautéed, 36–37
Onion, red, and Cucumber Relish, 140
Orange and Dill Pan-Seared Tuna, 153
Orange-Mustard Glaze, 152
Oven-Fried Chicken Nuggets, 139

P

Packets, Italian Chicken, 108–109
Pancakes, Zucchini, 188
Parmesan Perch, 160
Parmesan Puffs with Marinara, 39
Pâté, Easy Salmon, 15
Pea pods
    Honey-Mustard Turkey with Snap Peas,
      146
    Sesame, 190–191
Pear and Blue Cheese Triangles, 46
Peppers, bell
    Fiesta Chicken and Rice, 141
    Italian Steak and Vegetables, 74–75
    Nachos, 38
    Pizza Frittata, 58–59
    Stir-Fry, Three-Pepper, 194
    Turkey Tenderloins and Mixed Sweet, 143
    Vegetable Frittata, Spring, 56–57
Peppers, roasted, Red Pepper Bruschetta,
    44–45
Perch, Parmesan, 160
Pineapple
    Caribbean Chicken Kabobs, 116–117
    Glaze, Hot, 98
    -Lime Fruit Dip, 23
    Teriyaki Chicken Kabobs, 118

Pizza, Cheese, Family-Favorite, 178–179
Pizza Frittata, 58–59
Pork
    with Basil, Garlicky, 99
    Chops, Breaded, 92–93
    Chops, Greek Honey and Lemon, 97
    Chops, Honey-Mustard, 96
    Chops, Southwestern, 94–95
    Medallions with Hot Pineapple Glaze, 98
    Rich Vegetable Gravy with, 100
    Slices, Caramelized, 101
    Tenderloin, Caribbean, 102–103
    Tenderloin Crostini, Spicy, 32
    Tenderloin, Italian Roasted, 104
Portion size, 9
Potato
    -Basil Scramble, 52
    Green Chile and Egg Bake, 63
Prosciutto
    and Basil Chicken, 122–123
    Italian Frittata, Savory, 55

Q

Quesadillas, Spinach with Feta Cheese, 42

R

Recipes, carb values of, 210–211
Red Pepper Bruschetta, 44–45
Red snapper
    Creole, Grilled, 156
    with Mango Salsa, 155
Relish
    Corn and Tomato, 144
    Cucumber-Red Onion, 140
Rice
    Asian Omelet, 54
    and Chicken, Fiesta, 141
    -Vegetable Skillet, 182–183
Rubs
    Herb, 71
    Mexican, 71

S

Salads
    Asian Coleslaw, 206–207
    Bacon-Spinach, 199
    Caesar, Wraps, 176–177
    Chicken and Strawberry-Spinach, 132–133
    Creamy Dilled Cucumbers, 208–209
    Garden Vegetable, 184
    Greek, 200–201
    Greens with Fruit and Blue Cheese, Sherried, 202–203
    Italian Chicken, 120–121
    Lime-Mint Melon, 204–205
    Southwestern Chicken BLT, 142
    Vegetable, Garden, 184
Salmon
    with Orange-Mustard Glaze, Broiled, 152
    Pâté, 15
Salsa
    Chicken, Easy, 124
    Chipotle-Black Bean Dip, 48
    Fish Tacos, Grilled, 158–159
    Mango, 155
Sandwiches, Honey Ham Bagel, 66–67
Sauces
    Bacon-Dijon, 78
    Barbecue, 70
    Cucumber, 154

    Herbed Cheese, 50
    Maple-Mustard, 193
    Mint, Creamy, 106
    See also Dipping sauces
Sausage Breakfast Squares, Spicy, 64–65
Sautéed Olives, 36–37
Savory Beef Tenderloin, 82
Savory Italian Frittata, 55
Savory Shrimp and Scallops, 164–165
Savory Vegetable Stew, 181
Scallops, and Shrimp, Savory, 164–165
Sea bass, Gremolata-Topped, 148–149
Sesame Ginger Chicken, 110–111
Sesame Pea Pods, 190–191
Sherried Greens with Fruit and Blue Cheese, 202–203
Shrimp
    Gingered, 12–13
    Kabobs, Grilled, 161
    Nacho Bites, 34
    and Scallops, Savory, 164–165
    Southwestern, Stir-Fried, 162–163
    -Spinach Salad with Hot Bacon Dressing, 168
    Surf and Turf Kabobs, 31
    Thai-Spiced Cocktail, 33
    and Whitefish Cakes, 166–167
Sirloin with Bacon-Dijon Sauce, 78
Snacks
    common, carb/fat/calorie count, 215
    low-carb, 212
Soups
    Broccoli, Cream of, 185
    Tomato, Chunky, 186–187
Southwestern
    Chicken BLT Salad, 142
    Pork Chops, 94–95
    Shrimp, Stir-Fried, 162–163
Spicy Meatballs, 30
Spicy Pepper Steak, 80
Spicy Pork Tenderloin Crostini, 32
Spicy Sausage Breakfast Squares, 64–65
Spinach
    -Bacon Salad, 199
    Greek Appetizer Tarts, 20
    Greek Salad, 200–201
    Hot and Spicy Greens, 198
    Pie, Easy, 173
    Quesadillas with Feta Cheese, 42
    -Shrimp Salad with Hot Bacon Dressing, 168
    -Strawberry Salad, Chicken and, 132–133
    Vegetable Poached Eggs, 53
Spreads. *See* Dips and spreads
Spring Vegetable Frittata, 56–57
Starchy foods, common, carb/fat/calorie count, 213
Steak. *See* Beef
Steakhouse Sirloin au Jus, 76
Stir-fry
    Chicken, Summer Garden, 130
    Pepper Steak, Spicy, 80
    Shrimp, Southwestern, 162–163
    Three-Pepper, 130
Strawberries, -Spinach Salad, Chicken and, 132–133
Summer Garden Chicken Stir-Fry, 130
Sun-Dried Tomato and Bacon Bruschetta, 43
Surf and Turf Kabobs, 31
Swiss cheese
    and Ham Pie, Impossibly Easy, 60–61
    Honey Ham Bagel Sandwiches, 66–67
Swiss Steak, 79

T

Tacos, Fish, Grilled, 158–159
Tarragon Tomato Slices, 195
Tarts, Greek Appetizer, 20
Teriyaki Chicken Kabobs, 118
Thai Chicken with Cucumber-Red Onion Relish, 140
Thai-Spiced Cocktail Shrimp, 33
Three-Pepper Beef Tenderloin, 83
Three-Pepper Stir-Fry, 194
Tomatoes
    and Corn Relish, 148
    Soup, Chunky, 186–187
    Sun-Dried and Bacon Bruschetta, 43
    Tarragon Slices, 195
Tuna
    Orange and Dill Pan-Seared, 153
    Steaks with Cucumber Sauce, Marinated, 154
Turkey
    -Bacon Bites, 28
    Honey-Mustard with Snap Peas, 146
    Meat Loaf, 87
    Patties with Corn and Tomato Relish, California-Style, 144–145
    Tenderloins and Mixed Sweet Peppers, 143

V

Veal with Asparagus, 90–91
Vegetables
    Aioli Layered Appetizer, 40–41
    Beef and, Hearty, 81
    common, carb/fat/calorie count, 216
    daily servings, 8
    Frittata, Spring, 56–57
    Gravy, with Pork, Rich, 100
    Kung Pao, 180
    Pie, Impossibly Easy, 174–175
    Poached Eggs, 53
    -Rice Skillet, 182–183
    Roasted, Harvest, 192
    Salad, Garden, 184
    Steak and, Italian, 74–75
    Stew, Savory, 181
    Summer Garden Chicken Stir-Fry, 130
    See also specific vegetables
Volumetrics, 10

W

Waffles, Whole Wheat, 72
Weight loss
    balanced diet, 7–8
    exercise/activity, 9
    portion control, 9
    volumetrics, 10
Whitefish and Shrimp Cakes, 166–167
Whole grains
    common, carb/fat/calorie count, 213
    nutritional value, 7–8
Whole Wheat Waffles, 72
Wild Mushroom Herbed Chicken, 125
Wraps, Caesar Salad, 176–177

Z

Zucchini
    Pancakes, 188
    Spring Vegetable Frittata, 56–57

Complete your cookbook library
with these *Betty Crocker* titles

Betty Crocker Baking for Today
Betty Crocker's Best Bread Machine Cookbook
Betty Crocker's Best Chicken Cookbook
Betty Crocker's Best Christmas Cookbook
Betty Crocker's Best of Baking
Betty Crocker's Best of Healthy and Hearty Cooking
Betty Crocker's Best-Loved Recipes
Betty Crocker's Bisquick® Cookbook
Betty Crocker Bisquick® II Cookbook
Betty Crocker Bisquick® Impossibly Easy Pies
Betty Crocker Celebrate!
Betty Crocker's Complete Thanksgiving Cookbook
Betty Crocker's Cook Book for Boys and Girls
Betty Crocker's Cook It Quick
Betty Crocker's Cookbook, 9th Edition— *The* **BIG RED** *Cookbook*®
Betty Crocker's Cookbook, Bridal Edition
Betty Crocker's Cookie Book
Betty Crocker's Cooking Basics
Betty Crocker's Cooking for Two
Betty Crocker's Cooky Book, Facsimile Edition
Betty Crocker's Diabetes Cookbook
Betty Crocker Dinner Made Easy with Rotisserie Chicken
Betty Crocker Easy Family Dinners
Betty Crocker's Easy Slow Cooker Dinners
Betty Crocker's Eat and Lose Weight
Betty Crocker's Entertaining Basics
Betty Crocker's Flavors of Home
Betty Crocker 4-Ingredient Dinners
Betty Crocker Grilling Made Easy
Betty Crocker Healthy Heart Cookbook
Betty Crocker's Healthy New Choices
Betty Crocker's Indian Home Cooking
Betty Crocker's Italian Cooking
Betty Crocker's Kids Cook!
Betty Crocker's Kitchen Library
Betty Crocker's Living with Cancer Cookbook
Betty Crocker's Low-Fat, Low-Cholesterol Cooking Today
Betty Crocker More Slow Cooker Recipes
Betty Crocker's New Cake Decorating
Betty Crocker's New Chinese Cookbook
Betty Crocker One-Dish Meals
Betty Crocker's A Passion for Pasta
Betty Crocker's Pasta Favorites
Betty Crocker's Picture Cook Book, Facsimile Edition
Betty Crocker's Quick & Easy Cookbook
Betty Crocker's Slow Cooker Cookbook
Betty Crocker's Ultimate Cake Mix Cookbook
Betty Crocker's Vegetarian Cooking